SEARCHING FOR
DR. GOD

The Healing of a Soul

SEARCHING FOR DR. GOD

The Healing of a Soul

Sarah R. Taggart

ThomasMore®
– An RCL Company –

Allen, Texas

Send all inquiries to:
THOMAS MORE PUBLISHING
An RCL Company
200 East Bethany Drive
Allen, Texas 75002-3804

E-mail: **www.RCLweb.com**

BOOKSTORES:
    Call Christian Distribution Services 888-444-2524
    Fax 615-793-5973
INDIVIDUALS, PARISHES, AND SCHOOLS:
    Call Thomas More Publishing 800-822-6701
    Fax 800-688-8356
INTERNATIONAL:
    Fax Thomas More Publishing 972-264-3719

Printed in the United States of America

Library of Congress Catalog Number 00131623

ISBN 0-88347-453-0

1 2 3 4 5   04 03 02 01 00

ACKNOWLEDGMENTS

Although the title of this book is meant ironically, there are indeed doctors to whom I owe thanks. Erv and Miriam Polster, Doctors of Gestalt psychology, loosened my overly tight psyche and taught me to breathe. Psychoanalyst Sheila Mason taught me to value my inner self and helped to water my soul-garden. John Biersdorf, Doctor of Theology, formalized a new view of the physical universe and opened the door to the world of organized Christianity. Harold Edwards, Doctor of Religion, introduced me to psychosynthesis as a means of spiritual direction and became my friend and coauthor.

I offer thanks also to many spiritual teachers I met along the way. In particular I want to acknowledge Merriman Cunningim, Henry Lewis, Robert Werenski, Mary Lou Theisen, Walter Wink, Francis Geddes, Gordon Scott, Irene Hayden, Charla Khanna, and Lee Morical as especially valued guides. I am also inexpressibly grateful to the Religious Society of Friends (Quakers) for giving me an earthly glimpse of the Kingdom of Heaven, and to the American Roman Catholic Church, whose brave struggles I admire more than I can say.

Among authors who have influenced my thinking I should mention first and foremost C. S. Lewis, who introduced me (as he has so many others) to serious and uncompromising Christianity. William James dared me to exercise my will to believe. Lawrence LeShan, Fritjof Capra, Ernest Becker, and Freeman Dyson offered me new visions of reality. Rosemary Haughton, Frederick Buechner, Richard Rohr, David Steindl-Rast, M. Scott Peck, Gerald May, Diana Eck, and Tilden Edwards opened my eyes to contemporary Christian philosophy, and Jim Wallis, Morton Kelsey, John Sanford, Francis Schaeffer, Billy Graham, Teilhard de Chardin, and Hans Kung reminded me that Christianity has many voices and viewpoints.

I owe special thanks to John Purdy, Roberta Purdon, Sonja Page, and Linda McCarthy who carefully critiqued the original versions of this book. Above all, I owe thanks to the Olson family, who brought me into the church and continue to inspire, challenge, and sustain me through good times and bad.

C O N T E N T S

PREFACE

his is the story of a journey from death to life: death, meaning secular origins plus a long struggle with tuberculosis; and life, meaning faith and the church. It is also the story of one person's journey through the twentieth century; I was born in 1928 and so far am not dead.

My early indoctrination in secular materialism had a midlife collision with the New Age and in this account I present a case for some (not all) New Age precepts. I note that during the past fifty years we have moved from somewhat smug materialism to somewhat credulous spirituality and have also seen an increasing acceptance of psychotherapy, both New Age and otherwise. I describe the surprising role very good psychotherapy played in my passionate discovery of the church. Furthermore, although I did not travel the shortest route on my journey into faith, neither did God desert me when detours into social work and academia caused my frail faith to stumble.

In the Revised Standard Version of the Bible, Jesus is described as telling a story—a parable—about "importuning." He likens the Kingdom of God (he seems always to be attempting to convey the nature of the Kingdom) to the situation of a traveler attempting to wake a householder in the night in order to find shelter. The traveler is described as "importuning" the householder many times before the householder grudgingly comes to the door and lets the poor tired traveler in. The parable is baffling if one thinks of God as the householder—not so baffling when one realizes that God is the traveler.

The poet Francis Thompson describes God's importuning in his poem, "The Hound of Heaven," which begins with these lines:

> *I fled him down the nights and down the days;*
> *I fled him down the arches of the years;*
> *I fled him down the labyrinthine ways*
> *Of my own mind; and in the midst of tears*
> *I hid from him, and under running laughter.*

For anyone who avoided God as long as I managed to do, those lines have dramatic impact. In this account I recall my capture by the Hound of Heaven, and I revisit the arches of the years of my own life and the labyrinthine ways of my own mind.

I offer this book to old folks like myself who deprive themselves of religious comfort because they believe it to be irrational. I offer it to skeptical friends who identify themselves as "spiritual" but have no use for the institutional church, and to their opposite number, church friends who have lost their spirituality. I have resided in each of these camps at various times and I am convinced that church and spirituality inexorably belong together, because church without spirituality is lifeless and spirituality without church is baseless.

PART ONE:

The Country
of Death

CHAPTER 1

Swimming Upstream

One Sunday in 1941, my friend Alice Huntington and I emerged from a movie at Ann Arbor's Michigan Theater into the early dusk of a winter afternoon. The date was December 7 and I was thirteen years old. From the newsstand across the street we could hear a newsboy shouting, "Pearl Harbor bombed. The U.S. at war with Japan." We looked at each other in bewilderment. At war with Japan? Not Germany? And where was Pearl Harbor? But later, listening anxiously to the evening news on the radio, my parents and I learned that Pearl Harbor was in the Hawaiian Islands. The next day President Roosevelt gave his "day in infamy" speech and at that point our country was at war with Germany as well as Japan. Our familiar world was turned upside down.

But when one is thirteen years old, changes and frightening challenges loom everywhere, every day. A new house, the beginnings of sexuality, a certain independence from parental hovering—in other words, budding adolescence with all that implies of uncertainty and strangeness—had just dawned in my life. So the war seemed far away and existed primarily on the radio and in movie newsreels—or so I thought. But added to individual fears already accumulated through the years, its influence was apparently more powerful than I realized at the time. Sometime during that historic year, as I was waiting for sleep in my small bedroom, out of the blue came a vision of death as the absolute end. No me. It hit me smack in the gut. I remember a stomach-hitting-the-floor, heart-racing, dry-mouth panic, and after that first event the same panic seemed to recur over and over again: in the middle of the night, riding in the car, reading a book, waiting in the doctor's office. No me. Help.

After that, nothing ever scared me in the same way. But when I carefully touched on the subject with my parents, they didn't seem to know what I meant. "Don't worry about it," my father said. "When death comes you won't be aware of it." My mother tried to reassure me. "That's not something you have to think about for a long, long time." But, of course, I knew better. Setting aside the possibility that we might be bombed, which possibility seemed very real at the time, hadn't I learned in school that Calvin Coolidge's son had died after a blister on his heel got infected? Didn't children die of polio? Hadn't I once been in the hospital with a mastoid infection behind my ear that threatened to go into my brain? Kids die. I did need to think about it. Thereafter I became a hypochondriac on such a grand scale that every scratch, every sore throat, every adolescent lump threatened to do me in. And as if to prove a point, when I was seventeen I was diagnosed with tuberculosis and the dark ghost in the closet became a menacing specter in the room—more about that later.

But in the middle of wartime no one else seemed to be afraid of dying. Why was that? What did they know that I didn't? And, biggest question of all, what was the matter with me? "Hysterical" was a word I came upon at some point. "Overactive imagination." So I stopped talking about my fear and pretended that it had gone away. Afraid of dying? Who, me? Don't be silly. But when one is secretly preoccupied with a terror that seems to afflict no one else it is logical to conclude that one is crazy. That is what I concluded. I managed to hide my craziness under a facade of enthusiasm and competence: "the playground director" my mother called me when my competence turned into bossiness, as it frequently did. "A natural leader," said my teachers. But whatever they may have thought, I knew better.

Once in a great while I encountered vague reassurance. A high school English teacher, Marion McKinney, regularly left existential aphorisms written on a high corner of her blackboard, aphorisms sometimes addressed to the fear of death, as though she understood how scared I was (we were?). Even after all these years I can still recall one that gave me comfort: "That which is as universal as death must be a blessing." Many years later I ran into advice about facing death from the psychiatrist Irvin Yalom, a writer I had theretofore admired. Dr. Yalom recommended achieving objective distance — becoming preoccupied with other thoughts—as a way to deal with the terror of death. That was more or less what my family advocated. "Don't think about it; there isn't anything you can do about it."

But, as someone has whimsically observed, that is like saying, "Don't notice there's a tiger loose in the house." It became all I could think about. The famous photograph in Life Magazine of a dead American soldier in the Normandy surf after D-Day shocked me inexpressibly. A dead bird lying in my path on a walk in the woods was a terrifying reminder. Death was everywhere and yet . . . it was nowhere. The "objective distance" my family sought meant there were no funerals, no talk about death, and (in the midst of World War II) no one we knew seemed to die.

Eventually, I got a small amount of comfort from the realization that I was not alone with my death phobia. Once, when I was a social worker, the subject of death came up during a staff meeting. Our psychiatric consultant related fear of death to our insulation from actual dead people—to the absence of corpses in most of our lives. Huh? I remember looking around the room and noting that others also reacted with surprise. "It has nothing to do with corpses," my friend Sylvia retorted. "It has to do with nonexistence." But the psychiatrist persisted in his analysis and I could see that the room neatly divided itself into those who knew what Sylvia was talking about and those who did not. But, as was true of me, the others kept their cowardice to themselves, believing, I suppose, that they were alone among all those brave grown-ups who accept death as the end-of-life equivalent of birth. "If it doesn't worry you that you didn't exist before you were born, why should it worry you that you won't exist after you die?"

Earlier, my fear of death led to another neurosis. When I was in my midteens I discovered Christianity. I was attending a boarding school where chapel attendance was required every morning. Usually, one of the faculty gave a little talk about good moral character (rarely anything more religious than that), but one day a Christian evangelist slipped into the program. Among other things, he talked fervently about the Christian belief in resurrection. "You will live forever," he assured us, "because God loves you." If I would just believe in Jesus Christ I could live forever. Wow. Problem solved. But then, because I thought my fear of death was neurotic, I became equally ashamed of my attraction to Christianity.

For a long time after that boarding school sermon I hid my fascination with Christianity in approximately the same way I hid my fascination with sex. And the farther along in school I went the more persuaded I became that Christianity was just a sophisticated version of the fairy tales that educated people ("mature" people) should know better than to take literally. Christianity was a "mythology" similar to many other God-man mythologies with which, through the ages, the world had been peppered. I could go to church with my friends on special occasions like Easter and Christmas Eve, but otherwise I was well advised to keep my wishful thinking to myself.

Unfortunately, my death phobia did not decrease with subsequent maturity. When the by-now-familiar panic would hit me, as it regularly did through the years, I would say sternly to my inner self, "Think about something else." I muscled the oblivion aside, seeing it crouching in the shadows but able to march past it with fake bravado. Although eventually I began to have hyperventilation attacks—my heart raced and my breathing became shallow and I learned to breathe into a paper bag—there seemed to be no point in attributing those to my death phobia, over which I had no control and of which I was still ashamed. And I certainly did not want to be told that my Christianity, such as it was by then, was merely a defense I could learn to do without.

I found myself hiding my increasing fascination with Christianity from everyone I knew, like a love affair of which I ought to be ashamed. Whether I remained silent because I was standing in a grocery checkout line, or was chatting at a cocktail party, or was part of a larger group having breakfast or dinner together, I rarely took the bait when people offered ideas with which I did not concur. My environment was filled at that time with individuals who are now disparagingly labeled "humanists," though at the time I'm sure they thought of themselves as "progressive," whether or not they were also titular Christians, as some of them were.

"How can a person believe in a religion that teaches that it's the only one?" a close friend once remarked unbelievingly during our weekly breakfast together, having no idea that Christianity was an obsession of mine.

"I don't think God is a necessary idea in explaining the universe," my cousin's wife noted skeptically during a visit in California, when we got into a philosophic discussion about the nature of reality.

"Where was God during the Holocaust?" several Jewish friends have complained bitterly, suspicious as always of the motives of Gentile friends.

"How awful to say someone is 'in bondage to sin.' I think 'sin' is a terrible idea and I think any religion that tells me I am a sinner is a terrible religion. I have enough trouble with guilt as it is," said my daughter-in-law, defending her Christian Science education.

"Think of all the money people give to churches that could be spent helping the poor and preventing wars. What hypocrisy," my husband Herb used to state indignantly, being a pragmatist in all aspects of life.

Usually, such speakers supposed that I agreed with them, though Herb certainly knew better. I was frequently embarrassed that I did not, in fact, agree. What was the matter with me? Why did their comments and questions cause my stomach to knot up? Why did I continually seem to be swimming upstream philosophically, struggling with unanswered questions, tormented by an overactive imagination, haunted by intimations of answers just around the next bend? But I learned very early that if I tried to speculate about the reasons for our disagreements—to explain my reasoning—the topic would be changed and the conversation would quickly rise to the level of small talk.

Quietly, privately, hiding my books from family and friends, I searched for a doctor of medicine or psychology or philosophy who could magically open the door of understanding for me. When, by midlife, it became apparent that my questions about the meaning of life were taking me nowhere, I told myself somewhat ruefully that they were probably symptomatic of an embarrassing clutch of neuroses and fears which I, as a mature person, ought to be rid of. So after my children were more or less launched, I stiffened my resolve and determined to put my life to some useful purpose.

Then, after fifteen years as a social worker and college teacher—careers in which my religious impulses were sternly repressed—an unexpected miracle occurred. A new friend, my teenage son Bruce's accompanist, grabbed me by the elbow and insisted I come with her to hear Bruce play his French horn at her church. And then I went again the next week to hear him sing in the choir. And the next. And the next. Eventually, stifling my doubts, at age fifty-one I joined that church.

But while fear of death had devastated me in an instant, my true conversion emerged only gradually out of the rocky soil of my secular upbringing and education. It was not until I timidly enrolled in a doctor of ministry program, thinking I might become a spiritual director, that I finally stopped calling myself pejorative names and instead began to think of myself as an explorer and (a word someone later gave me) pilgrim. Through that creative program I came into what a later therapist whimsically referred to as "the Country of Life," and it was she who suggested that the wonderful image used by Jesus—"living water"—might be the truth for which I had so long searched.

2

A World Without God

My mother was a small person with a slim figure, perfect legs, and wavy dark brown hair. She bore a striking resemblance to the Duchess of Windsor, a resemblance that annoyed her because she didn't think the famously self-centered Duchess was particularly admirable. However, like the Duchess, Mother was meticulous in her approach to the world, neat to a fault and well organized in mind and body. She dressed every morning in carefully ironed underwear, silk stockings (nylons came in after WW2), a tailored dress or suit, and moderately high-heeled shoes. No doubt in an effort to create "ladies" out of her two teenage daughters, she sometimes emphasized to us that women students of her generation wore hats and gloves to class.

Mother was so meticulous that she almost never wore an apron, even when working in the kitchen, as she increasingly had to do. She came from a wealthy family and only began to feel comfortable about her wealth when she discovered the idea of noblesse oblige. The rest of her life was spent trying to live up to her noble obligations. She was a volunteer social worker when most social work was done by upper middle-class women like herself—no doubt my own eventual career choice was influenced by my mother's volunteer career.

Educational opportunities gave Mother the tools with which to master difficulties, so throughout her life she never stopped learning. When she found herself having a second child (Gretchen) when the first (Sarah) was less than a year old, she enrolled in a master's degree program in early elementary education. The John Dewey educational philosophy she then encountered—learn by doing, treat children with respect, use praise rather than punishment—caused her child-rearing methods to be rational, organized, and gentle, even though she also ingested some Watsonian behavioral ideas that were less nurturing—we were rarely picked up when we were babies ("don't reinforce crying") and lived on strict eating and sleeping schedules. Whatever my dad may have thought about these new-fangled theories, he went along with them because he respected my mother's intelligence and resourcefulness. He was, I realize now, a feminist before feminism was politically correct.

My dad was the other extreme from my mother, as am I. Big and tall, he had a large, open face, wore glasses and had lots of straight, mouse-colored hair. He was somewhat untidy, impulsive, full of stories (some of which were true), and was fond of babies and dogs. He had intensely loyal friends. He would sometimes laugh so hard he would fog up his glasses—I can remember him clearing them off with the big white cloth hanky he always carried in his pants pocket, at the same time wiping his eyes and catching his breath.

Dad grew up in Ann Arbor, finished two years of law school, and then quit to go into a variety of businesses at which he was never very successful. As a consequence of his mercurial career my parents did a great deal of moving around. For years Dad drank a martini at lunch and two martinis before dinner. He graduated to half a pitcher of dinner martinis when his health got worse late in life. I have concluded that he was by then an alcoholic but my husband insists he was just a heavy drinker, a distinction without a difference in my view. Dad also smoked a pack of cigarettes a day, which resulted in the emphysema that killed him at the age of sixty-nine. He and I had ferocious arguments about everything and I loved him with all my heart.

Dad always said, "Everything in life involves trade-offs." He and his tall, tough, smart, ambitious family (he was the youngest of seven children) were scornful of "that Roosevelt" because they thought too many handouts would make people soft and remove incentive from their lives. The trade-off for security and freedom from poverty would be laziness and irresponsibility. It was an odd paradox: although Dad himself was a good-hearted and generous person, he believed most people to be basically selfish and mean. Social planning seemed to him at best futile and at worst stupid; sensible people looked out for themselves and expected the worst.

Furthermore, my dad assumed that the world was a basically hostile place. The present-day gun mania and ubiquitous locked doors would, I assume, seem to him to be a logical consequence of the roaring twenties, the desolate and desperate thirties, and the wars of the forties and fifties. He himself carried a loaded gun in his car when he was selling insurance in Detroit during the 1920s, and when he was in his early forties during the Second World War he served for four years in the Marine Corps, with all that implies of weapons and killing. After he died we discovered a loaded gun in his bedside table.

When I was twelve years old Dad gave me a twenty-two rifle for Christmas and then set up a shooting range in my maternal grandmother's basement; I can remember my mother's fury, but Gram could never say no to Dad. You could hear the loud bang of every shot all the way to the third floor. On New Year's Eve, 1950, he fired a pistol into the air at midnight in front of our Arizona house to celebrate the half century. Dad liked guns and it would never have occurred to any of us that there was something wrong with owning and shooting a gun. "But the trade-off," I think he would now say, if he were around to notice, "is if you let us have guns, you're going to have to lock your doors."

However, while we did not lock our doors in the daytime fifty years ago, it is also true that we were not really safe either, though the dangers were isolated and less easily identified than they are now. When she was sixteen my best friend was kidnapped at the corner of Oswego and Hill Street in Ann Arbor, taken to the Arboretum, raped, and then returned to the front of her house. But there were no "rape happened here" slogans painted on telephone poles when we were young, and rape was a hidden menace; very few people knew about my friend's experience because she was told never to talk about it. Once, walking along South University Avenue in the early evening, I myself was stalked by a slow-moving car. With my heart pounding I hurried into Wikel's drugstore and phoned home, and that was the extent of my potential danger. But it was a warning I didn't forget. Thereafter I knew enough never to walk alone at night. I am somewhat bemused by modern "take back the night" campaigns, as though walking alone at night had once been safe.

These days I can see that danger has a salutary psychological side effect—that, in fact, life is supposed to be dangerous. A peculiar sort of evil occurs when we are too secure. We get comfortable and lazy. We become smug and self-satisfied. We congratulate ourselves and let the dust collect in the corners. Any sort of discomfort feels like a personal affront. Our lives become spent avoiding work, avoiding confrontations, avoiding failure. Let the other guy volunteer for the tough duty; why take chances? Why get married when so many people just end up getting divorced? Who needs to have kids? Kids are just trouble. Why can't old people call Dr. Kevorkian and die with dignity?

Don't misunderstand me. However philosophical I may be about danger and misfortune on an abstract level, on a personal level I am not volunteering to again undergo the mastoid operation I had when I was six. Let the critics object to the use of antibiotics for middle-ear infections; they forget that, before penicillin, an ear infection could spread into the mastoid bone behind the ear and, if not surgically dug out, could then seep into the brain. I can still remember how much it hurt when the doctor wheeled his little white enameled table into my hospital room every morning to change the dressing. Even though I was a very little girl, I can still feel that long strip of gauze being pulled out of the hole behind my ear. "You're such a brave girl," they told me.

I was not brave. Not then and not now. But in my family we did not complain. We straightened our backs and did our best when the going got tough. I was taught that a primary character fault was feeling sorry for yourself. If you were my dad, you cracked jokes. If you were my mother, you took naps. But you did not complain. You did not feel sorry for yourself. "It won't do any good," my mother used to say. Recently, after my sister's husband died an agonizing death, I broke down in tears at a cousin's house and was amazed to realize that I was embarrassing him. Feeling sorry for myself—even after all these years he had no way to cope with it.

Above all, no matter what was going on, you did not assume that some supernatural being would look after you. My parents considered the concept of God to be an idea that enabled humans to cope with danger and uncertainty but without scientific validity. "There is no evidence that anything, much less anyone, interferes with nature's laws," I was told. "We are animals, not essentially different from dogs and cats except that we have more evolution-arily advanced brains." The universe was held to be without beginning or end (a sentence without meaning if I ever heard one!). Evolutionary change was explained by the simple idea of survival of the fittest. Furthermore, life, apparently so special and on the surface so different from everything else, was believed to be merely a chemical anomaly that would eventually be explained scientifically. Life happens. There is no "reason" for it.

This agnosticism influenced our lives in subtle ways. For example, in our present home we have at least a dozen Bibles: old ones from my husband Herb's two pastor grandfathers, various translations acquired during my doctoral program, leather-covered ones, cheap paperback ones, even a tiny one that fits into my purse. And, of course, I couldn't resist spending sixty dollars for a concordance and an equally huge amount for the *Jerome Bible Commentary*. But in the various homes of my childhood there was no Bible.

Furthermore, the chasm between church people and my parents' circle of friends is, I am convinced, so wide that it is hard to adequately convey. Now that I live within Christendom I find myself shocked by my church friends' ignorance of the arid desert of the purely secular. Though the secular world is subtly pervasive in the commercial media (so-called Christian radio and TV stations seem to me to live in a world apart), I think many contemporary Christians hear its harsh message through the softening filter of their own unrecognized humanism. They fail, in other words, to comprehend the cruel philosophy behind such popular trends as abortion on demand and death with dignity. It occurs to me that the fundamentalists may be right about those things, and if I thought they were a little kinder (a lot kinder) about sexual politics in general and gay rights in particular, I would long ago have given in to my fundamentalist urges. Those of us who have actually lived in the world of the purely secular may have antennae that are lacking among many observant Christians.

But, on the other hand, I myself was equally ignorant about organized Christianity until as recently as twenty years ago. I thought Christians were naive, probably racially prejudiced, slightly silly, and not sophisticated in their understanding of the world. (Jimmy Carter, Ralph Reed, and Pat Robertson have certainly cured me of that last presupposition.) When I imagined life in churches I pictured church basement suppers with bad food, prissy ladies' aid societies, embarrassingly proper social events, and general ignorance about such important subjects as psychology and politics. Church people, I had been led to believe, were certainly not any fun.

Strangely enough, my grandparents all went to church. But they were "modern" Christians, Christians who believed in moral behavior and were slightly abashed by supernatural overtones. My mother in particular would get defensive when I alluded to her background as "secular." "I went to the Presbyterian Sunday school every week," she would indignantly remind me. Under those circumstances I wondered how she could know so little about what Christianity stands for, but if I managed to ask the question tactfully (never my long suit) she would laugh and start to sing "The Baptist Sunday School," which makes fun of Old Testament stories. "Please check your chewing gum and razors at the door and you'll hear some Bible stories that you never heard before."

Oddly enough, "God," taking the word in its largest sense, was absent from my early life not only because of the specific absence of religion but because of the absence of aesthetics in general, except as aesthetics reflected "good taste." Yet my mother was a naturally artistic person, and my father was from a family with musical talent. I suppose the result of believing primarily in knowledge as my parents did, rather than in the arts, is that artistic activities seem irrelevant, "a waste of time," in Mother's phrase. Dad was interested in making money and Mother was interested in civic good works. Moral people put their energies into furthering the social and material progress that seemed only to have been temporarily stalled by such inconveniences as two world wars and a major depression.

In my family's world, social responsibility replaced worship and the social sciences replaced the commandments. Morality was equated with kindness. It wasn't kind to disturb people when they were resting or working, nor to inflict one's emotions on others; "unkindness," in other words, was defined as anything that caused someone else discomfort or inconvenience. By extension, kindness meant that when my aunt and uncle became old and in poor health it was not kind to inflict their disabilities on others, so their mutual suicide was an entirely moral act within that frame of reference.

Kindness often conveyed bland conformity. "Don't be conspic-uous" was a corresponding commandment in my parents' ethical system, though why that was important was never clear to me; I suppose it had to do with "being nice." "She's not a nice person" called up a picture of someone with a loud voice and insensitive laughter. Words like "evil" or "cruel" or "greedy" were not in my parents' derisive vocabulary.

We did not use the word "love" in my family. Taken for granted was the expectation that parents and children cared for one another—certainly I was tenderly cared for. But "love" was equated with "sentimentality," and you were expected to conceal any "mushiness" behind a curtain of sophistication and competence. When I think of persons whom my parents admired—a psychiatrist friend, a professor in the law school, the volunteer social workers my mother worked with in various charitable causes— above all I am struck with their intelligence and self-control. As a result I was middle-aged before I could comfortably hug another adult, and hugging my young children occurred mainly as a form of reassurance when they had hurt themselves. These days I can feel their silent rebuke as my adult sons hug their own children and tell them that they love them.

In what way was the absence of God reflected in my parents' moral code? At some point in the gospels Jesus is asked how his true disciples are to be recognized. He replies that they can be recognized "by their fruits." By this, one assumes, he meant that the ultimate consequences of discipleship should be caring relationships, humility, bravery in confronting evil, a longing for virtue, and a willingness to reconcile differences. (I am, as you can see, reframing the Beatitudes.) Looking back I am particularly struck by the absence of humility in my parents' world. "Self-confidence" was positively equated with pride, and "meekness," as Jesus spoke of it, was an incomprehensible idea. I remember my mother saying dismissively, "Why would anyone want to be meek? You would just be a mousey person that people would take advantage of."

Above all, the idea of "sin" was rejected as negative and harmful. In the psychological world of my youth people were believed to be fundamentally good, and aberrations such as wars and murders were believed to be symptoms of collective mental illness. Or, at least, that's what my mother believed. My dad once told me that the fundamental philosophic difference between himself and his liberal friends (when you lived in Ann Arbor even died-in-the-wool Republicans like my dad had liberal friends) was his conviction that basically "people are no damn good." Of course, it goes without saying that such religious activities as confession, absolution, and last rites were savagely ridiculed by educated people of my parents' generation. How one was to deal with a guilty conscience never came into question because guilt itself was relabeled as ignorance and could be resolved by education and, if necessary, therapy.

This is a harsh and probably unfair assessment. My parents tried to be brave and kind. They valued honesty, self-control, responsibility, intellectual curiosity, good humor, generosity, and open-mindedness. One should be loyal and trustworthy. It was an early twentieth-century code of virtue for people who had been educated to believe in science. At its best this code of virtue reflected the gentle good sense of the early progressive education movement—good sense which governed the rational and thoughtful upbringing my sister and I enjoyed. At its worst it reflected a progressive humanism which earnestly believed that eventually science would rescue us from ignorance and create a brave new world.

CHAPTER 3

One War Ends and Another Begins

Northern Michigan was cold and buggy in the summer of 1945. At the National Music Camp, then as now known as Interlochen, the camp uniform (corduroy knickers, light blue shirts and navy blue knee socks), though oddly unfashionable, kept us covered and warm. Because of World War II the college division was predominately female; in our radio department were only two very young men, 4-F for reasons unknown. My dad was stationed in the South Pacific with his Marine Air Division service squadron. We had not seen him for seven months and knew only in general where he was located. The war in the Pacific raged on, though the war in Europe had recently ended.

And then one night everything changed. Founder and camp president Joseph Maddy stood on a table in the cafeteria during dinner. "Ladies and gentlemen," he said in an uncharacteristically loud voice, "I have an announcement to make." And so, on the evening of August 14, we learned that the Japanese had surrendered. "We just got the news on the radio." There was a long pause while everyone absorbed the truly amazing news, and then the clapping and cheering erupted. Later that night the entire camp population celebrated with a bonfire, an impromptu jazz concert, and a snake dance through the grounds. But it was a few days before the sense of unreality fell away. All the boys from my high school days had gone or were going in to the various armed forces. The war had been going on exactly during the years I was in high school; it began in December of my ninth grade year and now, as I was beginning college, it was done.

For four years the war had provided an ever present background for all our lives: on the radio every night, in the rationing of everything from meat and sugar to gasoline (we walked everywhere, or took buses), and in the presence of uniformed soldiers everywhere on the U of M campus. Above all, for me the war meant my dad's absence from our lives. Mother, my sister, and I had spent a summer with Dad at the Marine Corps Air Station at Cherry Point, North Carolina, and a Thanksgiving vacation at a small air base near Newport, Arkansas, but otherwise he was gone, and in the fall of 1944 he went overseas to a small island in the Pacific. We later learned it was called Engebi, part of the Eniewetak Atoll, and some years later it was blasted into oblivion by the early atomic bomb tests. Apparently, the planes for which his service squadron was responsible were to have taken part in the first wave of the invasion of Japan. But, of course, that never happened, thanks to the now much-maligned atomic bomb.

In spite of all that, I'm ashamed to admit that the suspense and horror of the war years was superseded by a private life so fiercely adolescent it nearly crowded everything else off the stage. A few years ago there was a movie about two little boys in London during the Blitz; the charm of the movie lay in its portrayal of kids creating fun out of chaos. Though our situation in the United States could in no way be compared to London—in many ways life was very normal indeed—as those little boys were typical children, so were we typical teenagers: self-absorbed, often unkind, ambitious, snobbish, mercurially emotional.

But added to the ordinary anxieties of adolescence, and in addition to the threatening presence of the war, there was for me an additional lingering shadow. I was always tired. Even as a child I had guarded my sleeping hours ferociously. I had several times interrupted adult parties with the tearful request that my parents and their guests not be so noisy so I could get some sleep. Athletic participation was torture because it depleted my stamina so much, an irony because I was a good athlete and was often asked to play in central positions. I particularly remember field hockey as impossibly strenuous; I would try to play goalie or be in one of the outside lanes. Tennis, that passion of my youth, would leave me almost sick with fatigue. Sleep-overs (we called them "hen parties") were a nightmare because invariably I was the nag who wanted everyone else to turn out the lights.

But it truly didn't occur to me that I was anything but just lazy (or fat and out of shape if I was feeling particularly self-critical). I was especially resistant to the idea that my fatigue was legitimate because I was impatient with my mother's persistent and unexplained tiredness, caused (I now believe) by lifelong depression. She needed to take long naps every day, so she over-napped us also. Out of our dislike of naps came the eventual assumption that normal people should not need such indulgences. Even the word "nap" had a nasty, boring sound. All through my early life, "Why don't you take a nap?" was Mother's typical response if I seemed in the least grumpy or out of sorts.

My chronic fatigue became truly disabling during my last year in high school. I had been at the Milwaukee Downer Seminary (a boarding school) the year before the Interlochen summer. It was at best an unhappy time. The seemingly unbearable tragedy of missing out on my senior year at the University High School in Ann Arbor seemed to me to be an unfairness from which I might never recover. So when I was tired at Downer I explained to myself that I was depressed. But oddly, long before Linus Pauling discovered the healing properties of vitamin C, I unexpectedly developed a passion for oranges. I can still picture myself in my room after school, frantically peeling navel oranges onto the newspapers I spread out on my desk, hardly able to wait to get them peeled so overwhelming was the craving. I would eat two or three at a sitting. Looking back I wonder if I staved off the final onslaught of TB with those oranges.

Later, at Interlochen, my long daily naps caused me to be a curiosity to cabinmates who, needless to say, did not nap. I was so exhausted so much of the time that I put myself on a training regime to renew my energy. As usual, I concluded that the fatigue was caused by laziness, and so every day I made it a point to swim out to the raft and back, not a long way by any means but certainly the limit of my endurance and swimming ability. I don't recall that it helped much. My impression, looking back after nearly fifty years, is that at Interlochen I got by on determination and effort, as I had done for much of my life. But apparently I had no sense that other people could cruise their lives in overdrive while I was still struggling to get out of second gear. Only recently have I started wondering what life would have been like if physical activities of all kinds had not been such a struggle.

In November of my freshman year in college I innocently went to the University Health Service because the bronchitis I had been contending with seemed to be getting worse. A doctor noticed on my chart that something had turned up on my university entrance X ray. She asked if I had had the X ray repeated as recommended. (Just imagine: every entering freshman at the university was subjected to a routine chest X ray, so common was TB in those days and so much a threat in communal living situations.) I was mildly worried but hardly alarmed; the doctor seemed to be more concerned that six weeks had elapsed without my being notified. She sent me upstairs for a quick X ray, and then home to nurse my cold. But soon thereafter the second X ray resulted in a much more serious reaction: I was invited to visit the seventh-floor tuberculosis unit of the old University Hospital.

Poor Dad. He had only been home for a few weeks when he was again cast in the role of emotional supporter, a role he played many times throughout my two long hospitalizations. Together he and I went up to the head resident's office, and together we and resident physician Fred Langner looked at the ominous X ray. To say I was terrified is to understate my reaction. I knew nothing about TB, though by the end of that day my medical education had very much begun. Dr. Langner gave me a small book to read, a book filled with drawings of cartoon TB bacilli that were, apparently, chewing away at my lungs. "You have a primary lesion," I was told. "Bed rest at home and we'll watch it for a month or so."

A month or so? I was enrolled in classes. I had a life. I couldn't go to bed for a month or so.

But my life was, at that point, out of my hands. On December 6, 1945, I went to bed at home, on the second floor at 2110 Vinewood Boulevard. I was seventeen years old. Though I was supposed to stay in bed except for bathroom trips, of course I was up and down. Friends came over and naturally my parents couldn't be in the house at all times, so in spite of stern instructions to the contrary, I would go down the flight of stairs to let people in and then up again to resume my invalid role. Mother had rented a hospital bed and turned over her large, bright bedroom to me during the day, so I entertained friends in style. But one vivid memory remains with me from my month at home: every afternoon I had a period of sweating. I blamed it on the afternoon tea Mother and I routinely had together, but afterthought suggests that maybe I was having the late-day fever so characteristic of TB.

It should have become apparent that the course of my TB treatment was to be steadily downhill when, after the Christmas holidays were over, it turned out that bed rest at home was not going to do the job. Soothed by reassurances about how this impending hospital stay was intended primarily to be a learning experience (that certainly turned out to be true), on January 2, 1946, I was deposited in an iron bed in a four-bed ward on the seventh floor of the University of Michigan Hospital.

That enormous yellow brick building, at one time the largest in Ann Arbor, was torn down a few years ago. I have always been sorry to have missed the day the wrecking ball did its work. After the building was gone there was a yawning emptiness on the Observatory Street hilltop, and the stunning view over the river as far as the North Campus was for a while finally open for all to see. We patients had occasionally glimpsed it through small back windows on the rare occasions when we were wheeled on stretchers to the north side of the building. How wonderful it was to gaze on the unobstructed vista in the open air.

Characteristic of the grimness of the old University Hospital was the fact that patients entered through the basement. At first glance it appeared that the entrance was a small, attractive, two-story stone building attached to the front of the immense thirteen-story institution. No such luck—that entrance was for staff only. When I drive down U.S. Highway 23 these days and catch a glimpse of the women's prison near Milan, I think to myself how much more like a prison the old hospital was than the modern campus I can spy through the barbed wire enclosure. The prisoners there can walk around, which we were not allowed to do, and can even visit with their children, which patients with children also were not allowed to do. And, of course, the prisoners get out of bed every morning, and go to the bathroom, and take showers and use the telephone. It seems hard to believe that we were permitted none of those ordinary activities. We were in bed. Period. Twenty-four hours a day in bed. Bedpans. Bed baths twice a week. Hair washes every other week. No TV, no crafts or handiwork, visitors for one hour once a day. Whatever they called it, it was more prison than any prison I ever heard of.

1946 was, of course, pre-antibiotics. I wonder how we would have felt had we known that within less than a decade TB would become relatively curable. Even at that point TB was the great scourge, the white plague, the second-leading cause of death in the world. My maternal great-grandparents had lost three of their four adult children to TB, including my grandfather, a fact not known to me until many decades later. We assume I contracted the disease from Gram, who had calcified lesions in her lungs, probably once active though she was never made ill by them. ("Don't you dare ever tell her that," warned my doctor, a longtime admirer of my grandmother. "She doesn't need to blame herself for something she didn't even know about.") I first had a positive TB skin test when I was four years old and I can faintly remember having an X ray at that time; I remember being promised it wouldn't hurt. But X rays were primitive in those days; you had to be really sick before something would show up.

Nevertheless, I have no doubt that I had TB off and on throughout my childhood.

The severely restrictive regime being enforced at the University Hospital had been invented by an Ann Arbor doctor, John Barnwell, a TB survivor himself, who concluded that if rest was the cure, absolute rest should be the perfect cure. So he devised a demonic scheme that patients miraculously were willing to endure, a testimonial to the power of fear of death. After all, we weren't chained to our beds! Yet as far as I know we all obeyed the rules as best we could; I can only think of one or two patients who were rumored to get out of bed when the doors were shut. The rest of us just lay there, and lay there in as close to a supine position as we could manage. Our beds were never cranked up and we were provided with only one pillow.

Why didn't we go crazy? My husband claims that my hospital experience is analogous to his army experience, but I have always maintained that it was very different indeed because in his situation everyone else was doing it also. But though my friends in the outside world were not, in fact, "doing it," very soon the hospital itself became my world and I was surrounded by shipmates in the same boat. Some people did go crazy though, and there was a ward at the Ypsilanti State Hospital for patients with TB. I remember when a woman in the room next to ours was punished for all the screaming she did by a trip to the state hospital (or so we assumed). Whenever I felt too depressed or restless or scared, I remembered her experience and attempted to keep my feelings under control.

In general the patients on the seventh floor at the University Hospital were remarkably sane. In the first place, we felt fine. TB had no symptoms until one was, so to speak, in extremis. Although we each had a small cardboard "sputum cup" on our bedside stands ("just in case") I never knew anyone who did much coughing. With the advent of the X ray, TB was generally caught and treated before coughing became the diagnostic red flag. However, people did die fairly regularly; the nurses would go up and down the hall shutting doors when someone died, so we always knew about it unless it happened in the night. And some forms of TB were uniformly fatal: tubercular meningitis, for instance, and miliary TB (of the blood). As we had blood tests every month we suspected we were being checked for miliary, so that was something else to worry about.

In a paradoxical way, the condition of the world in 1946 was a comfort in itself. I have no memory of my first acquaintance with the word "holocaust," and I suspect the word was not in general use until at least a decade later, but I surely do remember newspaper photographs of concentration camp survivors, and we heard about starvation throughout the world in the wake of the sudden peace. All of those horrors allowed us to rationalize about how much worse our lives could be under other circumstances.

After I had been in bed for six months, a decision was made to let me begin to get up. The routine involved having the patient sit on the edge of the bed for five minutes a day for a week, then sit in a chair for five minutes, then gradually increase the time until eventually she was allowed to walk a little. But after my first five-minute period in a chair, my TB "broke down." That is, the X ray showed increased disease. (A TB lesion never really goes away, it merely becomes encased in a calcium shell and is thereby inactivated.) That setback was, for me, the bottom of the pit. I suddenly realized in a way I never had before that I might never get well.

I was to remain on total bed rest for another eight months, but eventually I was cautiously allowed to try getting up again, and this time it worked. In September 1947, I finally was discharged: surely one of the two or three happiest days of my life. But seven years later, immediately after my son Jeff was born, my TB broke down again and I was readmitted to the hospital. I would endure another thirteen months in bed and eventual lung surgery to remove the recalcitrant lesion. The surgery revealed that I had not one but two lesions ("cavities," which were much more serious than simple primary lesions) and also involvement of my bronchi. I also began a rigorous program of chemotherapy during this second hospitalization: streptomycin three times a week (the usual dosage elsewhere was twice a week; once again the University Hospital went to extremes), which caused my ears to ring and my lips to tingle but which by some miracle had no lasting effect either on my hearing or my balance. I also took twenty-four PAS pills every day (para-amino-salicylic-acid) which gave me murderous heartburn and resulted, I am convinced, in a lifelong acid reflux problem. But whatever the side effects, the TB was for all practical purposes cured.

I know now that the second hospitalization itself, and probably the surgery, were unnecessary. A sympathetic intern once said to me, "I would go through this routine once, but you can believe I would never do it twice." The urge to escape never left me; on any number of occasions I fantasized getting out of bed and running away. That second time I had left behind a brand, new baby and a very upset two-year-old, as well as a new house under construction and a husband who was just starting a new job. In spite of the heroic assistance of Herb's mother and an angel housekeeper-nursemaid named Hermina Lutz ("Miss Lutz," as we always respectfully called this older Lutheran farm lady), it was a terrible year for Herb and a worse one for Steve, my two-year-old, who, judging from snapshots that were taken that year, forgot how to smile.

About ten years after my final discharge from the hospital in 1955, I learned that a drug I had not yet taken, isoniazid, seemed to guarantee complete remission of tuberculosis. So for a year I took a prophylactic dose of INA, as we called it, and finally became a healthy person. Earlier, before I agreed to lung surgery, I had promised myself that I would have another child (Bruce was born in 1958) and I would learn to ski. I achieved this beautiful third son without complications, and after the INA regime I felt free to ski, to return to tennis, to buy a bicycle, and in general to forget about my lungs. I have often observed that I have lived two lives. Until I was thirty-five I was, before everything else, an invalid. After thirty-five, my real life began.

4

Slightly Sane

When I was a girl I believed that craziness was the end state of a defectiveness continuum, "well adjusted" being at the healthy end, "neurotic" in the middle, and "crazy" at the sickness end. When you began to slide down the slippery slope toward mental illness the message was clear: you should have been paying more attention to your mental hygiene.

This philosophy became particularly menacing when, as a hospital patient, I began to realize that my mental health was being monitored. Casually dropped comments by nurses and others caused me to suspect that psychiatric consultants were controlling my life. Good adjustment for a fully immobilized bed patient evidently meant no tears, no irritation with roommates or staff, no restless resentment of too many months in bed, and, above all, no ancillary symptoms like sleeplessness and heartburn. And as a particularly hurtful psychological insult, during the second hospitalization I was told that the psychiatric consultants advised minimal contact with home so that I could become acclimated to my "new environment." So the covert visits with two-year-old Steve became controlled by the doctor's assessment of how upset I seemed to be afterward—my subsequent adjustment, so to speak. But never did I lay eyes on any psychiatrist. Not only would contact with me have involved exposure to TB, "therapy" (meaning psychoanalytic therapy) was out of the question because I could not then "work through" the neuroses that might appear.

By the time all this psychological correctness was finished with me I was experiencing serious paranoid thoughts. Every day our psychological adjustment was noted in our hospital charts; we knew this because occasionally someone would say, "I see by your chart that you were upset yesterday." That caused me to begin observing and assessing myself and my native talent for calling myself names became truly acute. I worried that people were staring at me, that they gossiped about how strange I was, that somehow I was so conspicuously neurotic that I would be classified as mentally ill. I was terrified of the idea of the state hospital, which was bandied about jokingly as the place I might end up if I was not cooperative.

Only my newly awakened religious faith kept me slightly sane. Two of my roommates had been raised in religious families and their beliefs had a big impact on me. I asked them questions. We had religious arguments. And in 1946 and 1947 a young hospital chaplain conducted regular church services for us, a singularly brave thing to do because it meant wheeling our beds into the big solarium so that he could conduct a proper service for a "congregation." One day this chaplain preached a sermon about prayer. How to pray. It had never occurred to me that there might be a methodology for prayer. Here was a professional person telling me that not only was prayer not childish, as I had suspected, there was a way to do it.

In addition, at that time the Sunday worship service from St. Paul's Episcopal Cathedral in Detroit was broadcast over WJR radio. Those broadcasts eventually became the highlight of my week. I learned to follow along, repeating the responses and whispering the traditional prayers in concert with the voice from the radio. Now, fifty years later, I can still recite from memory many parts of that service; what a disappointment it was when, during the 1980s, I attended an Episcopal service and discovered that the old prayer book was no longer in use.

In addition to the comfort I derived from my radio-inspired religious faith, I was further inspired by the communion services brought every month by roommates Jeannie and Rose's priests

(Episcopal and Catholic). I found myself fascinated by the whole procedure (though I did not see much of Rose's communion because Father Bradley always pulled the privacy curtain around her bed). But Henry Lewis, the Episcopal rector and old friend of my parents, would often sit by my bed and chat after he gave Jeannie communion. So one day I raised the possibility of receiving communion myself.

"You have to be a member of the church," explained Reverend Lewis gently. "But that might be a possibility."

"Wouldn't I have to go to confirmation class?" I anxiously inquired.

"Don't worry about it," he told me. "I'm sure you know enough." Then he thought for a minute. "Why is Easter on Sunday?" he unexpectedly inquired.

I had no idea why.

"Because the Resurrection occurred on Sunday."

Oh.

"There, now you've been to confirmation class," he said with a whimsical smile, and that, for the time being, was the extent of my ecclesiastical education.

One additional obstacle then appeared. "You've been baptized, of course." No, my parents did not believe in baptism. "Well, we'll have to do that first," Reverend Lewis declared confidently. "I'll speak to the bishop the next time I see him."

So a few weeks later Bishop Page, dressed in full regalia and accompanied by my parents and Reverend Lewis, appeared at my bedside on a Sunday afternoon and baptized me. Several Sundays after that the bishop reappeared to confirm me into the Episcopal Church. It saddens me to realize how few details of that afternoon I can remember. I suppose I also received a first communion and I suppose Jeannie's family was also there. It had been a huge decision, my first step into what would prove to be the mansion of my true life. I could not have known on that incredible afternoon that my life was changed forever.

But my religious beliefs continued to be simple and uninformed. I knew nothing about the Bible and no one thought to give me a Bible when I was confirmed. (Looking back it occurs to me that Bible study would have been a wonderful addition to my life in the hospital.) Nor did I know very much about what Christianity in general stood for, other than that we should love one another. I had picked up what I suppose most liberal Christians pick up, a sort of euphemistic kindliness derived from those radio sermons and from the quasireligious novels that were popular at that time. Incomplete though it was, it was not bad theology, and I even acquired an elementary concept of sin and confession, the consequence of living with a committed Catholic. But the subtle complexities of the Christian faith did not enter my life until many decades later.

After I got out of the hospital at the end of 1947, my parents decided to leave Ann Arbor and move West. Dad's job had not worked out and it was believed that a new start in the bright, dry air of the desert would be good for me while I convalesced. Grandmother Riggs, who had traveled widely in the West, recommended Tucson as a healthful and lovely place (in those days it was a small university city) and so, less than three months after I returned home, we three—Mother, Dad, and I—moved to Tucson. (Gretchie was at that point in college in Ann Arbor.)

My parents hoped that I would find friends at the University of Arizona, but my "up time" allowed me to take only one class and I had no idea how to behave in a college atmosphere where I had nothing in common with other students. Three days a week I walked the two blocks to the university, attended class for one hour, and walked home to bed. I hardly exchanged a word with another student; I lived in a cocoon of loneliness. Recognizing my misery, and knowing how much the religious experiences in the hospital had meant to me, my dad encouraged me to go to church in Tucson; he even offered to go with me if I felt too conspicuous going alone. But I got the impression from him that church was an acceptable crutch if I wasn't strong enough to do without it, and this time it didn't help. The church service itself is a blurred memory, though I do remember summoning up the courage to go to a Sunday evening gathering in the nearby Episcopal student center. It was a disappointingly strange experience; among other pieties we were expected to kneel on a hard wooden floor to pray. That was too much spiritual ardor for me—I never went back.

And my hospital-generated faith did not prove to be sturdy enough to survive a secular education. It did weather an unhappy freshman year at Pomona College in Claremont, California, thanks to Merriman Cunningim from whom I took my first significant Bible class, and whose chapel sermons comforted me when depression threatened to overwhelm me. But when I re-enrolled in the University of Michigan in 1948, I once again found my faith assaulted on all sides. I occasionally attended St. Andrews Episcopal Church, but my college friends were not church people and I had the irrational idea that my church attendance betrayed a latent mental illness. I even thought that people observing me sneak into St. Andrews would see that I had not made a good adjustment to life in the real world.

I had transferred to the University of Michigan in order to reconnect with Herb Taggart, with whom I had had a brief romance the previous summer. A veteran of World War II service in Iran and Italy, Herb was attending the university and living at home with his parents and sister. In June 1950, we were married. For the first year of our marriage we lived in married student housing, I continued to take a limited number of courses with a major in English, and Herb completed work on a master's degree in educational counseling. In 1951, Herb accepted a teaching job in a suburb of Detroit, and in April 1952, our son Steve was born without complications of any kind. But it was an exhausting life for someone who had spent five years more or less in bed, and I had neither energy nor time for frills like religion, especially because religion didn't interest Herb.

My true conversion—the knock on the head that allowed the Hound of Heaven to capture me—came during the second hospitalization after our son Jeff was born in 1954. Somewhere during those desperate first weeks Doctor Nancy Furstenberg took a chance with an unorthodox bit of proselytizing. She wheeled me on a stretcher into an empty examining room so we could talk privately. She told me that she was concerned about me. "Is there anything we can do for you? Any way we can help?" Then she looked away and I could see her debating with herself. "You know," she finally said, "when I was in college my roommate died of polio. I haven't talked about this very much to anyone, but it really frightened me. In fact"—and I could see her embarrassment as she shared this—"I eventually joined the Catholic Church."

I murmured something about being sorry and that that was interesting.

"Do you have any religion?" she asked me hesitantly.

I told her about my baptism and confirmation eight years earlier (though I suppose there must have been something about it in my big fat chart, so probably she already knew). "But I'm a backslider," I admitted. "I haven't been to church in a long time."

"Would you like to talk with someone about all this? Henry Lewis maybe? Shall I call him for you?"

I agreed, and after a few days the Reverend Lewis once again came to call. I can still picture him, a tall, handsome, white-haired man in a black suit and clerical collar, somewhat stooped, carrying an armload of books. He was the very image of an Episcopal rector. (Handsome as he was, he eventually survived three wives!)

"Well, Sally," he said with sympathy. "Here you are again." (He always called me by my mother's name and I found it so touching I never corrected him.) He asked me briefly about my religious life and then said, "I've brought you some reading matter." He handed me three books: *The Case for Christianity* by C. S. Lewis ("If you haven't read it you might start there") and two books of Christian apologetics. "The word means 'argument in defense of the faith,'" he explained. "I'll come back next week and we can discuss what you've read."

I hungrily read the C. S. Lewis and, of course, because I had lots of reading time available, I read it carefully. Then I read the apologetics books. Suddenly, I had an intellectual framework for a faith I so badly needed and deeply longed for. When Reverend Lewis came back the next week he brought more C. S. Lewis books: *The Screwtape Letters, The Great Divorce,* and *The Problem of Pain.* I have no memory of the details of our discussions but Reverend Lewis was right, C. S. Lewis was the perfect place to start because he anticipates the reader's skepticism. One finds oneself pulled into his line of reasoning without a jarring note. My mind became persuaded, though it was a long time before intellectual understanding was again united with practice.

And intellectual understanding did not provide a substantial enough rock on which to build my house of faith after I got home. Fear of death and the haunting sense of myself as neurotic were stronger than ever. My home environment was still aggressively secular; I even acquired a new friend next door, a warm and eloquent psychologist who presented the case for scientific skepticism in such compelling terms that my doubts were again rekindled. So during the years my children were growing up I slipped back into the secular world in which I had been raised and to which Herb stridently belonged. Though I continued to be obsessed with religious ideas and questions, I still did not belong to a church.

Indeed, I was again vaguely embarrassed to be thought of as a "Christian." Nowadays a person such as I was then would be described as "spiritual," but that was not part of our vocabulary in those days, except as it suggested someone who read palms and tea leaves. Sometimes I prayed, I secretly read religious books, I displayed Sister Corita posters, but it seemed less confining, even less corrupting, not to be identified with those dogmatic, mildly ignorant others who went to church.

5

Weeding The Garden

In 1964, after my three sons were reliably in school (Bruce was born in 1958), I again went back to the University of Michigan. After laboriously finishing a bachelor's degree with part-time classes only, in 1969 I earned a master's degree in social work. Then for ten years I worked for a private family and children's service agency in Ypsilanti, Michigan, doing counseling and casework of every conceivable kind. It was work I loved and was good at, but restlessness eventually overtook me. I got tired of fighting society's wars for the pittance the agency called a salary. I got tired of running up against the same old dead ends: self-aggrandizement masquerading as professionalism and diagnostic guesses masquerading as knowledge. And another obstacle started to appear: I found myself beginning to think of clients in categories (another depressive, another sociopath, another passive-aggressive) rather than as individuals. Furthermore, I was not interested in climbing the agency career ladder and my private practice was becoming seductively large, taking more and more of my time. So one spring day I announced to my supervisor that after my summer vacation I would not be back.

But no sooner had I quit my agency job than the phone began to ring with messages from friends at Eastern Michigan University. The social work program there had just been awarded a huge government grant and they immediately needed to hire four new faculty to teach courses in family and children's services. Was I interested? Apparently, I have a short memory; maybe I thought teaching in college would be different from teaching second grade, which I had briefly done earlier and hated. At any rate I said yes, and for the next four years I worked harder than I have ever worked in my life. The first year at Eastern I had ten—count 'em, ten—new courses to prepare for. I learned a lot, but the main thing I learned (again) was that I am a lousy teacher and so, when the department quite appropriately declined to put me into a tenure track position, I again abruptly quit. I had no future plans. I only knew that I had taught my last class at any level and that I was doing myself and future students a favor by getting out of there. Without any sense of what to do next, I slammed the door on my social work career.

As I look back I realize it was the watershed decision of my life, although of course I did not know it at the time. When people asked me what I planned to do next I said, "I'm waiting." Waiting for what? I didn't know. I had a formless conviction that something would turn up and I had made up my mind that until it did—until I was shown a clear path to follow—I would do nothing. I still had some private clients and for several years I had had an urge to write. So I did marriage counseling for a few hours a day and the rest of the time I sat in a big white naugahyde chair in our living room, and on yellow legal pads, using ballpoint pens, I wrote two novels.

I was, at that point, fifty-four years old. All three sons were living elsewhere, Herb was still counseling junior highers as he had been doing for nearly thirty years, my father and grandmother were dead, Herb's mother was dead, and Herb's father was to live for only two more years. We were becoming the older generation. Within six years all three sons would be married and soon grandchildren would cast us in new roles. But for now I seemed to be thrown back into an overdue adolescence. My self-identity was fluid and shaky and I had the characteristic midlife sense of foreshortened time. Menopause cranked up my emotions along with my body temperature and I seemed to be exploding with dissatisfaction and fervent longings. And most distressing of all, I began to have vivid, mystifying, and recurrent dreams.

Finally, one winter night, while on a skiing vacation with two friends, my loosened feelings coagulated into a blockbuster nightmare, and in the small hours of the morning I was slammed awake by this dream. I debated with myself whether to go into the bedroom where the others were sleeping so I would have someone to talk to, or to sit in the living room until daylight, trembling with fear and sorrow. I decided that the terrible feelings would pass—that I could figure the dream out and make the feelings go away—so I waited in the cold and dark for several hours until my friends finally sleepily appeared.

Both of them were psychotherapists and they listened silently as with (by then) wooden feelings and dry mouth, I narrated the long dream. In the dream I was in a bare hospital room where my only entertainment was to be a computer. I realized that I might be there forever. I was trying to escape when a doctor-friend who resembled my father appeared. He put his arm around me and said he was sorry. He offered to find help for me, but first he told me he needed to see some other clients. He then went into a small, cozy room where I could see the family with whom he was working: a little girl sat on his lap in a rocking chair and in a corner a crippled young man lay on a balance-board. Through the door (I was standing in the hall) the doctor called out to me that he had heard that my mother was about to marry someone and begin an exciting life far away. I was filled with despair and began to weep. Then, still weeping, I woke up.

As I write this down it doesn't seem so bad. But even now I can still see the big, cold, bare hospital room and remember the small hope that the familiar face of the doctor-father meant rescue, hope that was dashed when he left me for those other people, with the chilling news that my mother was to have happiness that would be denied to me. We could all interpret the Oedipal content in that dream; I don't remember that we discussed it much. What struck my friends was the fact that never once did I use the word "love," even though it was clear that the doctor in some sense loved me. It was such an arid place, such arid relationships—stuck forever in a hospital room with a computer, while somewhere else there was life.

After we talked for a while, one of my friends asked me about therapy. "I don't know," I said. "I guess the right therapist has never come along."

"Who are you waiting for?" she asked. "Sigmund Freud? If you wait for the 'right therapist' you'll never do it. Open the yellow pages and throw a dart. Call someone."

So when I got home I called Dr. K., a psychiatrist whom I had used as a consultant in my own practice. I liked him because he was genuine. No baloney. I guess I must have sounded desperate because he asked if I needed to see him right away. "No," I said. "It'll wait till next week." But I felt warmed by the offer.

If I take a clinical look at what was going on I can see that I was in a midlife crisis. My age was right; I was by then fifty five. The circumstances were right; life had knocked me off my feet and immobilized me. "I feel as though I am stuck in the mud, spinning my wheels, unable to move." Not a bad description of depression, but at the time I didn't call it depression. I only knew that I was miserable. I saw Dr. K for eight months and then, since my marriage seemed central to my misery, my husband and I went together for another six months or so. I began to feel better, more in control, and because things were somewhat better with my marriage, and because I no longer seemed depressed, we terminated the therapy.

But meanwhile, in another compartment of my life, a startling change occurred. My lifelong fascination with poetry, philosophy, and religion—with the meaning of life and death—had culminated in my officially rejoining the church again, after many years of a more and more secular existence. I came back to God through what seemed to me then, and seems to me now, to be a mysterious set of coincidences. The Hound of Heaven, chasing me down the years! God, as my friend Charla likes to note, is sly.

My return to the church happened in a way I could never in a million years have predicted. Through their friendship with my son Bruce, I fell in love with the Olson family. That is not too strong a phrase. They were as different from my family as I could imagine, yet Mary, the mother, became almost a sister to me, a friendship which continues to nourish and sustain me even now. Not only did she cajole me into going to church with them, she cajoled Bruce into attending a Lutheran college (St. Olaf) and in 1981, to my astonishment, I became a Lutheran. It was relentless missionary work of the most basic kind.

It still amazes me to sit in a circle of people and talk about God. For years God had hidden between the covers of my books, or in my whispered prayers in the night, or in a journal where I imagined that God spoke to me through my writings. Though God seemed oddly present, God was an embarrassment. I once told this to Dr. K., hoping he would help me explore this facet of my experience. Instead he said sheepishly, "You know, when the word 'God' appears, my experience is that psychological types get acutely uncomfortable." And that was the end of our discussion of my religious life. After we terminated, I wrote him a frustrated letter filled with angry justifications of my beliefs. I made an analogy to talking about political beliefs with which the therapist may not concur. Why, I wrote, is it not the same thing? Of course, I realize now it is not the same thing; religious experiences are much more ineffable than fact-ladened political opinions. But at the time the hardheaded skeptic from the desert of my mind was ever lying in wait to ambush me, and my hand was ever on the pistol-grip of logic.

I dove into organized Christendom like a thirst-crazed survivor. I loved the hokeyness of the Christmas pageant and the ladies' circle and the potluck suppers. I loved the extra concerts that the choir gave on Sunday afternoons, and I loved watching the patient children sitting with their coloring sheets in their parents' pews during the sermons; I'm sure one reason that their church is so deeply imbedded in the personalities of most Lutherans is that it became part of their subconscious awareness at such an early age. I even loved most of the sermons; after all, I had not been listening to sermons since I was three so I was not tired of them yet. Above all I loved communion, filing soberly down the side aisle, kneeling before the altar as the pastor said the magic words and gave me the flat little wafer and the sweet red wine, walking self-consciously back up the middle aisle with my hands clasped reverently together and my eyes cast solemnly down, listening to the choir singing anthems as I sat in prayer, waiting for the others to finish. When two of my sons became members of that choir, it seemed to me that my joy was complete.

But one thing bothered me. During coffee hour and at church circle meetings I noticed that there was very little real personal contact between people. It occurred to me that Lutherans ought to let down their hair, put up their feet, and get acquainted; in other words, should shed their Scandinavian and German reserve. So when the associate pastor approached me with the suggestion that I put my social work experience to work, I optimistically helped him to organize small groups in the personal-growth style I had learned in my other life as a Gestalt therapist and teacher of social group work. There was apparently a need for this, because after a slow start the small groups became more successful than I would have imagined, and the friendships that were fostered are still important in the lives of many of the participants.

One of the serendipities of those small groups was my fascination with stories of other people's relationships with God. I began to accumulate new friends with spiritual tales to tell. One of these turned out to be a niece of ours from Ohio, who found herself staring down a series of blind alleys in her search for a vocation after she finished college. After a number of long conversations it became clear that her religious life was central in her considerations. Finally, she decided to go to divinity school, and later, during an overnight visit, she revealed that she had been accepted at both Harvard and Yale divinity schools and didn't know which one to choose.

I found myself having mixed feelings. Of course, I was thrilled for her, but in my heart I could feel a pang of sorrow. What was that all about? It was familiar. I had felt it on other occasions: when I visited with new friends who lived on a seminary campus, when I heard people talk about church camp experiences, when I participated in simple table grace in people's homes, when I heard about church retreats. After our niece left I was sitting at my kitchen table pondering my reaction when suddenly it hit me.

I was jealous.

I have since heard this description of how God answers prayers: the answers come in those small thoughts which are loaded with feeling, but which are so fleeting that we usually overlook them or dismiss them as unimportant. This time I managed to grab the thought before it dissolved, and as quickly as I had hold of it another was added to it. "You don't have to be jealous. Do it yourself."

I was staggered. I could go to divinity school? But where? How? Why? I picked up the phone and called a friend who had spent her life as a campus pastor's wife. "Martha, meet me for lunch. I have a crazy idea I need to check out with you. You know everybody in the world of religious education. Maybe you can help me." Martha and I sat over lunch for more than two hours; her preparation for the sociology class she was supposed to teach that afternoon remained undone. I babbled on and on in my excitement and she was both sympathetic and encouraging.

"But," she told me, "there are no seminaries in southeast Michigan. The nearest place is probably Chicago." At that point I was not to be discouraged. "Then I will commute to Chicago," I said recklessly. I had no idea how a theological education was structured. Would I get a master's degree? A bachelor's degree? No degree? And what would I do with this education? Though I hadn't the vaguest idea, I realized I didn't even care.

Suddenly, Martha's face brightened. "I am remembering something," she said. "Last week I interviewed for a teaching position at a new place in Detroit. I think all they offer is a doctor's degree, but that might be all right. The catalog is in my desk at home. I'll tell you where to find it." So that was how I found the

Institute for Advanced Pastoral Studies. I rushed home with Martha's catalog and a door to a new world opened as I read the description of their curriculum. It sounded so perfect for me that I felt giddy. I quickly typed a confused and excited letter to John Biersdorf, the director. Several days later I had a phone call from him. "You don't exactly sound sure of what you are looking for," he noted. "Why don't you come in and talk with us." So I did, and it is a testimony to my motivation, to what seemed to be God leading me, that that experience only increased my certainty.

At that time the Institute was located in the Sacred Heart Roman Catholic Seminary in the heart of inner city Detroit. Going there was like revisiting the Middle Ages. The huge building was nearly deserted; when I finally found the correct corridor there was no one in sight and I sat on a chair in the hall like an obedient child, waiting for someone to appear. Finally, an athletic-looking, middle-aged man in khaki pants and a sport shirt arrived, walking slowly and carefully. He introduced himself as Jack Biersdorf and warned me that he was just recovering from surgery and was still uncomfortable. He led me into a deserted room and proceeded to lie down on a huge beanbag chair positioned in the middle. Not knowing where he expected me to sit, I perched primly on a wooden chair nearby and looked down at him as we proceeded to conduct an extremely odd interview.

He had a deep, soft voice and most of the time I could barely make out his words. I didn't want to keep saying "Pardon me?" so I missed much of his half of the conversation. However, because I did most of the talking it didn't really matter, and after a while he indicated that he wanted me to speak with one of their students, "a woman very much like yourself," who was there from Wisconsin for a seminar. He led me down miles of damp echoing hallways— the seminary seemed to have no students—and I wondered where on earth this "seminar" was being held. Finally, we heard a few voices and Jack Biersdorf disappeared through a door, to appear a minute later with a tall, dark-haired woman about my own age who was red-eyed from weeping.

"Do you mind talking with this lady?" he asked her, gesturing at me.

"I think I'll be all right," she replied. "You'll have to excuse me," she said to me, wiping her eyes.

That was my introduction to Lee Morical, who was finishing her first year at the Institute. Writer, teacher, "priestess" (her own amused word), friend, later to be monthly roommate and mentor, I would never have taken the plunge had it not been for her impassioned testimony on that day. She later recalled that she was upset from an emotional experience in a healing seminar and didn't think she made much sense. But she spoke so directly from the heart and was so committed to the Institute program that I was persuaded somewhere beyond the level of reason.

One of my strengths seems to be a willingness to wait out chaotic situations in the conviction that eventually the pieces will fall into place. So I spat in the face of common sense and enrolled in this confusing program. I felt irrationally attracted to the promise of a self-directed curriculum consisting of prayer, meditation, monthly "colleague group" meetings, six major research projects, and a dissertation leading to a Doctor of Ministry degree.

The Institute For Advanced Pastoral Studies (now called the Ecumenical Theological Seminary) became for me a sort of "narrow gate" opening into a world I never knew existed. If the Lutherans handed me the ticket to what a subsequent therapist called "the Country of Life," the Institute provided the map and the transportation and above all the trip itself. I found God in huge new dimensions. I eventually found whole communities of life-giving people: Cursillo, St. John's Seminary, a Spiritual Guidance Intensive in Kansas, Shalem, Pendle Hill, Four Springs, classmates and carpool partners, and, most importantly, the Immaculate Heart of Mary Sisters at Visitation, in Monroe, Michigan, as I will describe in a subsequent chapter.

Unfortunately, and in spite of my new adventures in the Country of Life, the Country of Death was still there, buried deeper and deeper in my subconscious. I still had trouble sleeping.

I still found myself weeping for no particular reason. My legs still ached mercilessly and I still had nightmares and other wildly vivid dreams. Furthermore, I still found myself unable to find vocational direction, to know what to do with my crazy new education. And the dramatic culmination came when my marriage again seemed to be collapsing. So at that point I was back on the proverbial sinking ship, this time without a clue as to where to find the life jackets.

However, in the back of my mind was tucked a comment that an old friend and colleague had made when she heard about my problems. "You don't have to do this all alone." That again. She reminded me about Sheila Mason, from whom I had once taken a course and whom I had discounted as too reserved, too formal, too psychoanalytic. "She has walked on life's pebbles," my friend said. "She's the only therapist who's right for you."

I managed not to rationalize to myself that all I needed was God. Maybe I had given myself that message in the past, but it seemed clear to me that God sends helping others and that we are expected to use our relationships as fully as we can. So while I was doubtful that Mrs. Mason would understand my religious proclivities any better than Dr. K. had done, I was not worried that I was somehow being irreverent. However, I was determined to be utterly candid about my religion from the very start. No euphemizing. No using secular words to soften the blow. (That turned out to be harder than I thought. Somehow the phrase "talking to Jesus" came out "the words I hear in my mind." It was many months before Jesus' name made it into my therapy.)

The turning point came after a year or so (these encounters truly take a long time!) when, at the end of a session filled with my exasperated sarcasm about psychologists who explain away religious beliefs, Mrs. Mason remarked mildly that I seemed to have fallen in with an awful lot of reductionists. She noted that religion can't be explained away by examining its origin in one's personal history. "It's much more than that, isn't it?" she commented softly.

Why should that have changed everything? Because it was true. The image that pops into my head is a rose that is examined by plucking it out of the ground, versus a rose that is watered and left in the sunshine to flower. Indeed, garden images were important throughout our time together. Mrs Mason once likened therapy to the weeding of a garden, so that one could then see what wanted to grow. "What God has planted" would be my way of saying it, but she did not use God language. Still, I became increasingly comfortable with my own God language, and my own religious imagery became increasingly explicit.

Someone has remarked that too often therapy seems to be an endless voyage with no destination in mind. In my case, a goal appeared very quickly and remained in sight throughout the two years in which I saw Mrs. Mason twice a week. It helped me to know a goal was there; I felt more optimistic and motivated. The goal was the recovery of feelings that I long ago had repressed as too painful and dangerous, allowing them to reappear in transformed ways in my present life.

The word "transformed" is important. This was not an exercise in catharsis. More and more I began to realize that my transformed feelings reappeared in my religious life. As I was increasingly facile with religious imagery, I rediscovered more and more of my deep and profound emotions. No longer did I experience my life in watertight compartments: my religious life over here and my everyday life over there, with no communication—or only defensive communication—between them. The old repressed feelings provided the manure, so to speak, and sometimes very teary water, but God planted the seeds and continued to provide the sunshine.

The encounter with Mrs. Mason occurred simultaneously with the beginnings of my doctoral program in Detroit, and the two experiences proved to be mutually illuminating. At the same time that Mrs. Mason was weeding my soul-garden, my new education was enlarging my intellectual understanding. As a condition of enrollment, and because my master's degree (an MSW) was in the wrong field, the Institute people required me to take some theology classes at the nearby St. John's Roman Catholic Seminary. "You will not find their Catholicism to be a problem," I was assured, and indeed I did not. Furthermore, I was allowed to choose my courses, so I took three Bible courses, an early church history course, a course called "Foundations of Theology," and an existential philosophy course. Suddenly, my passions and my intellect found themselves joined.

The teaching in that place, largely by Catholic priests and nuns, was as excellent as any I have experienced anywhere—in fact, it occurred to me that my own teaching would have benefited by their example. During my two years at St. John's I found friends who shared my interests, I widened and deepened my religious knowledge, and a new world suddenly opened up to me, the larger world of organized Christendom. Of all the life-changing outcomes of my pilgrimage, the time I spent at St. John's Seminary seems to me in retrospect to have been the most miraculous.

I managed to stretch out what could have been a three-year program into six years, largely because my research took a long time. When I first began I said to my son Bruce, "Ye Gods, I'll be sixty by the time I finish this thing."

"Mom," Bruce reminded me sagely, "you're going to be sixty anyway."

6

Politically Incorrect

The four years teaching at Eastern Michigan University were, in some sense, a no-mans-land in my life, dividing "the Country of Death" from "the Country of Life"—the secular from the religious. So I want to describe those years in more detail, because at EMU I unexpectedly confronted the confusing morality of secular academia.

Pray-Harold Hall, where my first office was located, turned out to be a metaphor for the whole EMU experience. It was a perfectly square building with entrances at each of the four corners. There was no way to tell from the inside which entrance you would find yourself coming out of. I would absentmindedly go out what I assumed to be the door to the parking lot and find myself on the sidewalk to the Student Union. And because my office had no windows, it was hard to orient myself. I had no sense in that building of where I was or where I was going.

Luckily, I had a charming Australian colleague, Peter Bleby, who noticed me wandering around in a daze during those first weeks and gave me wonderful advice. "In a new job," he told me, "I always give myself six months to be totally stupid. I figure they won't fire me in that length of time, and I can ask all the dumb questions I want without getting into trouble." But even asking questions turned out to be a problem. Everyone in the social work department seemed to talk in code. Conversations were conducted with multiple acronyms and I quickly discovered that one-upmanship was the name of the game, one-liners and obscure references being the weapons of choice and victory apparently going to the smartest person in the room.

Eventually, I began to understand the rules of the game. Teaching was assumed to be a snap. ("The easiest job you'll ever have," a colleague told me.) So when teaching turned out to be very much the hardest job I had ever had, I was ashamed to ask for help. I had no idea how to write a syllabus (an unfamiliar term), construct an exam, understand the grading system, or organize a three-hour class. Or, most dismayingly, how to use the library, which had turned electronic since I was in school. Furthermore, I discovered I was expected to put together "course packs" (copied excerpts from my own library) rather than assigning university library reading, because many university books had pages stolen out of them, or faculty members had them squirreled in their offices, making the library relatively useless. I also learned that students always had the upper hand because a punishment for being too hard on students was called "being grieved," meaning that students could file grievances with the university. There would then be hell to pay. "Don't flunk anyone," I was advised. "You don't want to be grieved."

But above all I began to catch on to unspoken intellectual norms—political correctness, as it has come to be called. Occasionally, I heard references to "academic freedom," but by and large I got the impression of a rigid set of concepts that any intellectually up-to-date person should accede to without question. References to women and minorities were to be unfailingly positive, and woe to you if you inadvertantly made a negative comment. Religion was an obsolete superstition, an amusing anachronism. Also, dismayingly, public school teachers were frequently ridiculed as ignorant obstacles to good case management, and because I knew of Herb's warm concern for students I found this a particularly hard pill to swallow. It was assumed that virtually all human problems could be solved by good public policies, and remaining problems were probably caused by inadequate funding. If you disagreed with any of these concepts the sharp tongues of your colleagues were guaranteed to keep you in line.

We were, in 1979, a social work faculty of ten people. But there were relevant splits among us. Two were closeted gays (one eventually "came out" to me, an honor I value to this day), two were loudly defensive ex-clergy, and as a group we were divided almost equally between militantly liberal (secular) and timidly conservative (religious). But in spite of our private convictions, and even though the overall ethos of a public university is supposed to be religiously "neutral," we laughed uncomfortably when, as frequently happened, jokes were made about God. ("God will get you if you do that," someone would say facetiously, or "God told you to say that, right?") What neutrality meant, I noticed, was that there were to be no discussions in class or elsewhere about the positive role of religion in life. On the other hand, it certainly was okay to bring up negative religious influences. An Alice-in-Wonderland environment existed at EMU, ruled by the Red Queen of political correctness.

We represented ourselves as professional experts, but it soon became apparent that odd bits of ignorance masqueraded as expertise. For example, the colleague who for years taught our sexuality course once told me indignantly that we had no homosexuals on our faculty. "How do you know?" I asked her. "Because, Sarah, if someone does not tell me he or she is gay," she asserted, "I assume they are straight." "But why would someone tell you something like that?" She had no answer. Her acquaintance with alternative sexualities evidently did not include the realization that these were usually closely guarded secrets for some good and practical reasons.

I myself was guilty of acting as though I had more knowledge than I did. In most of my courses that first year I was the proverbial one chapter ahead of the students. "You have had all that experience with clients," said the friend who recruited me into the job. "Think of all the case examples you have at your fingertips." But case examples did not substitute for academic knowledge. I have a nightmarish memory of myself sitting in the conference room in the Monroe County courthouse, pretending that I knew something about social work in a court setting. "Have you ever gone to court with a case?" I was asked during my initial job interview. "Of course," I said confidently, remembering all those adoption and foster-care cases. But taking a case to court, and knowing how courts operate and why, proved to be entirely different concerns.

I was equally ignorant about public welfare departments, where I was supposed to help students do "family therapy" with selected cases. In one such department a kind and competent service director with the unlikely name of Bob Smith tactfully provided me with a much needed education. In another, however, the service director recognized my ignorance, stuck me at a desk in a utility closet (literally), and ignored me as much as possible.

But there were a few bright spots. At EMU the students were a godsend. At first I assumed that intellectual challenges would be the highlights of my time there, and I was mildly afraid of the students: working class, often middle-aged, often black, frequently with direct service experience in nursing homes, prisons, welfare settings, and mental hospitals. I felt sure they would have my number the minute I opened my mouth. What I discovered to my surprise was that the students were bright, tough, mature, and generous. What's more, at EMU my latent racism was challenged when some of my smartest and most sophisticated students turned out to be black.

I mentioned earlier that I doubt that church people understand how harshly the world is viewed by the strictly secular. My four years at EMU crystalized this perception. As a beginning social work instructor I was told to teach "social work values" to my students. I was genuinely puzzled. What was a social work value? Values, it seemed to me, were values; everyone knows what "values" means. A Boy Scout is trustworthy, kind, loyal, helpful, friendly, courteous, cheerful, thrifty, obedient, brave, clean, and reverent. What other values would one have in mind?

"Thou shalt not steal, lie, commit adultery, dishonor your parents . . . (all ten commandments)." Doesn't that about cover it?

Wrong. Social work values were built upon a concept called "self-actualization," meaning full development of the client's individual personality, and included the ability to keep client secrets (confidentiality), respect for individual differences, and freedom of choice. All this sounds very moral until one considers practical outcomes.

I think of a gentle, gracious black lady, Mrs. R, probably in her midsixties, living in a small twenties-style frame house on the near west side of Detroit. Her ancient mother was due to come home from a convalescent hospital after recovering (more or less) from a stroke. Her husband was dead and there was a retarded son also living in the household, which barely got by on various social security checks. I was doing a discharge planning assessment for the hospital.

We sat with our tea in china cups on her glassed-in front porch, amidst a jungle of houseplants, while Mrs. R. courteously and carefully sketched out her life for me. I began to perceive the presence of a truly sainted soul and I was embarrassed to realize that I had come with the intention of "intervening." But Mrs. R had no doubt encountered more than her fair share of social workers and she was too polite to imply that I might be butting in.

After a while I asked about her church connections. "I am a Christian," she said tactfully. When I then asked how her faith influenced her ability to cope with this difficult situation, she said serenely, "I don't think of it as a difficult situation. I am serving the Lord when I take care of my family. It is a privilege." My genuine interest must have then shone through because Mrs. R. spent the next half hour or so explaining her religious beliefs to me. It was a wonderful education.

Was Mrs. R's personality being actualized? I suppose so, in some sense. Certainly her soul was being actualized. But soul actualization was not part of our social work values system. Mrs. R. was practicing love in the most elemental way, but I'm not sure that my colleagues really believed there was such a thing as sacrificial love, speaking psychologically. They spoke of self-sacrifice like Mrs. R's as "masochism" and accepting care from loved ones as "manipulation." One should not interfere with a son or daughter's self-actualization if a parent has had a stroke—the parent should go to a nursing home. But it occurs to me that if "self-actualization" is the ultimate psychological goal, then the Red Queen is truly in charge and Moses and the Boy Scouts have some reconceptualizations to undertake. Under those circumstances it is hard to know what moral door to use (to get back to my original metaphor) except that selfishness is apparently a reliable guide.

Recently, when I took care of several grandchildren during a hard time in their parents' marriage, a friend said grimly, "You'd better watch out." Meaning: You'll be stuck with those kids if you aren't careful. I was so shocked that I forgot to be tactful. "I'll do what I have to do," I retorted, and my friend had the grace to be embarrassed. But she was merely reflecting a popular psychological concept, "codependency," meaning taking on someone else's burdens in an effort to be helpful, and in the process causing that person to become dependent on you. But what that also implies, as far as I can see, is that one should mind one's own business and look out for number one. (Yes, I know that "codependency" originally referred to situations where one person's care-giving fostered someone else's helplessness instead of relieving it. But it soon became generalized to include justification for selfishness in many other circumstances.)

In contrast to self-development as a moral goal, I have memories of my mother-in-law. I hold her up to myself as a standard of moral behavior, an example of soul actualization. In a cheerful and friendly way she extended herself for others, even though she had a rheumatic heart that caused her extremities to swell and her heartbeat to be frighteningly irregular. For years after she died I would meet Ann Arbor people who, on hearing my name, would ask, "Are you related to Jessie Taggart?" Her competent good nature was honored by an amazing number of people. But she was not a martyr—it was not self-sacrifice for the sake of self-aggrandizement. "We do what we have to do" was a phrase she gave me as she made yet another half-day drive to check on an elderly aunt-by-marriage. She cared for my two-year-old during my last TB hospitalization. She cared for her own mother during her mother's last, bedridden days, and she was the only person who managed to get along with her difficult father-in-law. ("I think I was the only person who liked him.") But she also recognized the limits of sacrificial giving. "If I ever tell you that I want to live with you, you are to assume that I'm senile," she told me with a smile, remembering how difficult her mother's illness had been for her. But, as it turned out, the diagnosing of senility was never necessary because Jessie Taggart died suddenly at the age of sixty-nine. I still miss her. I wish she were here to meet the lovely great-granddaughter who bears her name.

I do not mean here to condemn social work in general. I remember my earlier social work years with pride. When my son Bruce would tell people I was a "marriage counselor" (one of several hats I wore), I would correct him. "I am a social worker," I would insist. "I'm not ashamed of the label." While I was doing direct service work—counseling, child welfare and group work—I know that I helped people to cope with life more successfully. My colleagues at Child and Family Service were compassionate, appropriately modest, and knowledgeable. We established bonds of genuine affection with many of our clients. So my anger at social work refers to the theorists, not most of the practitioners. "Abandon common sense all ye who enter here," should have been the motto of the EMU social work department, and four years of teaching there highlighted for me many problems I had previously only glimpsed.

When I finally, hesitantly, ventured into the world of organized Christianity, moral questions began to receive simple, common-sense answers and life's purpose gradually began to make sense. Instead of four doors leading nowhere, I passed through the proverbial "narrow gate," and ahead of me lay the Blessed Community, the Kingdom of God.

PART TWO

On A
Pilgrimage

Taking Chances

I have never been interested in being "sensible," a label that got hung on my sister early in life. Since childhood I have been attracted to the mysterious and eccentric, so sailing off into the unknown as I began to do in midlife not only did not seem scary or weird, it seemed reflective of my true self. Waiting out the chaos at the Institute for Advanced Pastoral Studies seemed no more irrational than had an earlier encounter with something called "Gestalt therapy." When I enrolled in a two-month-long Gestalt therapy training program, I had no idea what I was getting into, but for some reason it didn't worry me. "I'm a big girl," I told friends and family. "I can always say no."

I realize that anyone meeting me for the first time would probably be surprised by all this. My "persona," as the Jungians call the face one presents to the world, is solidly conventional. During my various adventures I sensed that an unspoken question, "What's that dumb, middle-aged housewife doing here?" hung in the air wherever I went. Or worse. "I'm going to have to deal with that bitch one of these days," admitted a new friend about his initial reaction. "You certainly aren't like the impression you first give."

I tiptoed into what later came to be called "the New Age" in 1973 at a daylong Gestalt workshop in Detroit. The workshop itself was slightly dull, but afterward I was aware of a feeling of well-being that seemed somehow connected to the odd experiments we had done. The following summer I enlarged the experience with a three-day Gestalt workshop in Ann Arbor. It proved to be marvelous; all kinds of lights went on in my head. The basic philosophy seemed to the taking of responsibility for oneself in the present moment, not a revolutionary idea by any means but certainly at odds with the retrospective sorts of therapies I had previously learned. So when I later received a brochure from the Gestalt Training Center of San Diego, it occurred to me that I could stay with my mother (who was then living in San Diego) and take part in the monthlong training that Erv and Miriam Polster were by then offering on the West Coast.

What did I learn from the Polsters, who turned out to be the sole faculty in this training program? If I think of times when my basic personal philosophy shifted, those two summers I spent in San Diego would be high on the list. While the philosophy was entirely secular, I learned above all about the value of taking chances. Every day we were invited to participate in the risky emotional experiments that are at the heart of Gestalt therapy. I can still hear Erv's deep, nasal voice asking, "Would you be willing to try something?" I learned not to be afraid of my emotions and not to discount my power.

Erv taught us that Gestalt therapy is a three-legged stool resting on awareness, contact, and experiment. In other words, it stresses the importance of the present moment, the healing properties of intense contact with another human being, and the bravery required in getting out of the stuck emotional places in which each of us is frequently trapped. I also learned that integrity, openness, compassion, and humor offer remarkable benefits in the healing process, and I discovered that I did not need to compromise my personal values, even if the group in general held values different from my own. Furthermore, Miriam Polster became for me a model of feminine warmth, wisdom, depth, and aesthetic knowledge (she is a singer, among other talents). Some years later, when I went back for a few hours of personal therapy with her, my respect and fondness were reinforced.

After that first Gestalt summer I decided to act on another experiment that had previously intrigued me but had seemed too eerie and far-out to try. I decided to learn Transcendental Meditation, then in its heyday. And to my surprise, because he was impressed by the changes wrought by the Polsters, Herb agreed to go with me. Transcendental Meditation promised that it would cleanse our minds of extraneous chatter so that life experiences would become more vivid and fruitful. In what I later learned is a basic Buddhist idea, TM proposed to enable us to achieve an emotional detachment which would result in serenity and new understandings.

The TM classes turned out to be lessons in the use of a "mantra," a meaningless word which we were to run repeatedly through our minds with the goal of eventually being "without thought." That "without thought" notion seemed senseless to me at the time, since awareness of no-thought itself struck me as a form of thought. But I now believe that "thoughts" and "awareness" are two different mental states and that my understanding was limited by the English language. (I gather that Sanskrit says it better.)

There was great secrecy associated with one's mantra, which was "given" to each of us by the teacher and which one was never supposed to reveal. Unfortunately I hated my mantra, the word "keering," which sent my mind into mental cramps. In other meditative settings I have tried other mantras, preferably ones with open vowels, and find that these work better. Ironically, the best meditative technique of all has proved to be attention to my breathing, without any associated words.

In a similar way, my education at the Institute For Advanced Pastoral Studies enlarged and changed the way I viewed reality. Thanks to Jack Biersdorf's intellectual curiosity and teaching skills, the very foundations on which our core assumptions had been built were shifted. Jack's informal lectures, plus the readings we were led to—Fritjof Capra, Lawrence LeShan, David Bohm, and others—enabled us to view reality as (above all) stranger than we could ever have imagined. Among other things, Jack was fascinated by the apparent effect of the mind on the material universe. "Prayer has power we have never dreamed of," he once suggested, "because reality's essence apparently has consciousness as an ingredient."

Furthermore, Jack noted that matter and energy are inexorably affected by time and space, and therefore matter, energy, time, and space are probably different aspects of the same thing. He also suggested that because everything in the universe is interconnected, proximity is not needed to create cause and effect. "The universe does not operate like an automobile, in which the wheels must be attached to the axle, which must be attached to the car body, and so forth." Even more startling, it occurred to him that concepts themselves may merely be convenient ways of thinking about the unthinkable—metaphors masquerading as reality. It is an idea that still causes me to shake my head in wonder and that has profoundly changed my perception of the universe.

Jack was an ordained Christian minister, but I realize now that many of his ideas would now be derided as "New Age." He was an inquisitive person and he was continually trying out new ideas on his students. He conducted "rebirthing" experiments, was interested in crystals, reincarnation, and various body therapies.

He meditated frequently, and engaged in a form of yoga he called "morning practice." At one time he was deeply involved with addictive personality concepts and was explaining therapy in terms of the Twelve Steps. Yet he continued to practice Christian intercessory prayer and to offer formal weekly communion to his staff and students. He considered himself an active Christian and ran a predominantly Christian graduate program.

During my first year at the Institute, in yet another attempt to come to grips with my personal demons, I enrolled in Jack's weekly "Spiritual Care and Counseling" class. I hoped the class would combine religious practice with therapy of some kind. My months with the Polsters, and later with Sheila Mason, were wonderful in most ways, but a deep spiritual connection with God was missing.

However, Jack's class turned out to be a frustrating disappointment which eventually led to a serious disagreement between us. He was teaching a therapeutic technique called "neurolinguistic programming," a therapy that I found excessively mechanistic and very far indeed from spiritual care. When I challenged him about this, he told me that his view of therapy was to give clients "a new view of how their minds work so that they can discover their own solutions to their problems." He considered "good decision making" to be the key to mental health.

I was unclear at the time about why I disagreed so passionately. Mental functioning, it seemed to me, was already nourishing my personal demons. I did not need to pay more attention to my mind.

Week after week I drove through rush-hour Detroit traffic with tears barely contained, and week after week my anguish was ignored as we were invited to explore the different parts of our minds. I had a sense of my essential self being absolutely discounted and of being molded into a prejudged form by a rigid process—it was very unpleasant. I stopped attending when I realized that my discomfort was getting worse because no attention was being paid to my soul. Not until I sojourned in Kansas, where I encountered the psychological system called "psychosynthesis," did the full implications of my problems with Jack's class become clear. I concluded then that spiritual care has primarily to do with the relationship between one's essential self and God. It asks two questions: "Who am I?" and "Who is God?"

However, there was a serendipitous outcome from Jack's class. I became curious about what I later learned was called "spiritual direction." It would be a number of years before I encountered a formal definition of "spiritual director," but I realized that I needed to discover how, if at all, spiritual care differed from conventional therapy. Indeed, I thought when I finally finished this crazy doctor's degree I might hang out a shingle as a spiritual director. But at that time spiritual direction was so obscure that when a well-known campus pastor consulted me about it neither he nor I knew where to turn.

Finally, I decided to try to find places that advertised themselves as combining psychology and Christian spirituality in some way, without any clear sense of where or what that would turn out to be. But once I went public with my query, acquaintances began to suggest possible projects and locations that they had either experienced or heard about. I learned about a spiritual direction intensive in Kansas, a Jungian center in California, a school for spiritual guidance in Washington, D.C., a Quaker retreat and education center near Philadelphia, the spiritual renewal system known as Cursillo, and most intensively (and transformatively) the nine-month-long program of spiritual formation known as the Ignatian Exercises.

So yet again I took a deep breath and jumped in. My time with the Polsters, with the TM people, and especially with Jack had given me the courage to venture into the unknown. But I had absolutely no idea how I would be changed by these journeys, what the risks and temptations would be, nor where I would be when I was finished. It took me four years of traveling all over the country to find out, and in some sense my life was changed forever.

8

Catholic Connections

I have trouble recalling the days when Catholics were so foreign in my world that when a friend married a Catholic man, her family disowned her. In those days we had all kinds of biased opinions about the Catholic Church: authoritarian (yes, dear Catholic friends, I know you still struggle with that), anti-intellectual, rampantly superstitious, as well as an early twentieth-century prejudice (not entirely religious) against the Irish Catholics in Ann Arbor. So when I took my first class at St. John's Roman Catholic seminary, I was stunned to have my prejudices blasted away by the power of the intellectual ideas I encountered, and thereafter Catholics seemed to form a pivotal center no matter where I went.

It seems to me that the sly God is nowhere more sly than in the Catholic Church. A shortage of priests is giving new voice to the religious women in the church, and the nuns I met on my journey were a revelation: smart, sensitive, intensely faithful, incredibly brave. Furthermore, the dearth of religious vocations for both sexes means that there are lots of vacant convents and monasteries available for other purposes, so all but one of my workshops was held in a Catholic setting, and the two I will talk about here were explicitly Catholic in content as well.

CURSILLO

It was during a coffee break at St. John's Seminary that I first heard about Cursillo. "Kerseel" the attractive, red-haired woman called it.

We were having one of those polite conversations that one has with strangers with whom one is passing a few minutes of the day. She had asked me about myself and as usual my explanation left her puzzled; in a ten-minute break there is not time for a life history, so I explained offhandedly that I wanted to explore how spirituality and personal growth were related. Her face lit up and she threw that strange word at me. Then we went back to our synoptics class. The next week she again joined me for coffee and said she would bring me some information about whatever-it-was if I wanted her to. I asked her for more details (such as "How do you spell it?") and learned a little bit about what "it" was and where it came from. Ten minutes worth. This truncated conversation continued for most of a semester and finally I asked if I could participate in a Cursillo.

"No," she said. "Not unless you know someone who's already participated who could sponsor you."

I was appropriately discouraged. But the following week when we resumed our discussion my new friend sheepishly said to me, "I got to thinking about how dumb I am. Why else were you led to me if not to have me sponsor you?" She looked quizzically at me. "I don't really know you but it seems obvious that I'm to take the chance."

So I enrolled in the next "Women's Cursillo Weekend." The initial instructions were a bit worrisome. My new friend would take me in her car to the Sacred Heart Seminary in downtown Detroit on Thursday night, where she would then leave me. She would pick me up again on Sunday evening. I would not be able to contact my family except in an emergency. In other words, I would be stranded and alone. It occurred to me at that point to wonder what I was getting into.

The new Catholic Archbishop of Detroit was trying to discourage ecumenical endeavors taking place in Catholic seminaries, and so the twenty-five participants met up under the rafters on the top floor of the enormous old building which is the Sacred Heart Seminary. We slept on cots in the room which had at one time been the gymnasium. (There was, as a consequence, a plethora of showers!) I had taken plenty of warm clothes (the season was early spring) and instead it was as hot as midsummer for the entire weekend, so most of the time I was miserably hot. Except for our meals and a final, bootlegged liturgy in the main chapel, we never saw the rest of the building and never set foot outside.

Every moment of the three days was programmed. We spent most of the time sitting at round tables with five other participants and a group leader—four tables in all. The programmed portion of the weekend took the form of talks to the entire group on particular Christian subjects (love, hope, charity, anger, etc.) in which the personal experience of the speaker was shared. We were then invited to share our own personal thoughts and experience with that particular topic in our small group, and then draw it, or write it, or sometimes sing it, in order to make the experience more real for ourselves and each other. Periodically we would be interrupted by "palanca" time, palanca being cards, letters, and gifts which were sent to the participants by loved ones or by other Cursillistas who had taken responsibility for the weekend. Even though I knew no one except my sponsor, I received numerous small surprises. We were meant to feel cherished and indeed that was the response.

What are my principal memories of Cursillo? Ouch. I remember the hard chairs—we must have done a great deal of sitting! I remember the wonderful singing. The Episcopal priest who was one of our leaders had brought a small electronic piano and a tape deck, and every portion of the time was introduced and summarized with music and song. I remember my small group of women—such hard lives, such courageous sharing. The women were from all kinds of backgrounds and all ages (though I was one of the older women there). I was reminded anew of the power of the small group. As promised in the introductory letter, I remember the tears, my own and those of my fellow group members. The sharing was frequently both painful and cathartic. I remember the intuitive responses that developed between many of us. I remember the beautiful worship services in the tiny, primitive, makeshift

Cursillo chapel up there in the eaves, which the leadership had devised in defiance of the archbishop who was denying us the use of the worship facilities downstairs. The contrast between that empty, cold tomb of a seminary, where only a dozen or so seminarians were enrolled in any given class, and the vibrant, joyful, noisy Cursillo going on high above struck us all.

When I signed up for the Cursillo weekend I knew that I was flying under false colors. I did not have the time to make a genuine commitment to the Cursillo movement and, frankly, I was participating out of curiosity. I warned my sponsor that this would probably be the case, but she thought that the weekend itself might persuade me. However, I realized afterward that Cursillo is, indeed, a life commitment which would have subverted the direction my life was taking, and I did not follow through. So the full impact of Cursillo is not part of my own life. But I can see that not only has Cursillo been an important spiritual renewal movement within the Catholic community throughout Europe and the United States, it also has spread to the Protestant community, and Episcopal and Lutheran churches have developed their own versions of Cursillo. I am convinced that it is not only a process of spiritual renewal but of personal growth as well. Most of us came away from that weekend healed and affirmed in many areas of our lives.

THE IGNATIAN EXERCISES

I became acquainted with "The Nineteenth Annotation of Ignatius of Loyola" through an Immaculate Heart of Mary nun named Sister Nan, to whom I was referred after yet another workshop at St. John's Seminary. She was skeptical when I first inquired about the Ignatian exercises.

"Do you know what they are?" she asked me.

No, I didn't.

"Have you heard of Ignatius?"

More or less. I knew that Ignatius of Loyola was the founder of the Jesuit order and had been a soldier.

"You are a Roman Catholic?"

No.

"Have you ever heard of the Nineteenth Annotation?"

No.

"Why do you think you might want to do this?"

Good question. Because I had heard that whatever this was, it combined spiritual direction with personal growth in some way.

"Have you ever been in spiritual direction?"

No, but I was in psychotherapy.

That last elicited a frown. "You understand that this will be a very rigorous program. You will meet with a spiritual director once a week, and every other week you will also meet for several hours with a group of other people undergoing the exercises. You will commit yourself to at least one hour of prayer a day, to assigned scripture reading, and to the keeping of a journal. Do you think you would be prepared to do that?"

Yes.

"I should warn you that Ignatius was a military man and some of the exercises are in military terminology. Also, because they are from the fifteenth century, some of the wording is very sexist. Will that bother you?"

I didn't know. I was prepared to find out.

"Well," she said with a small smile, "since you seem to have been led to us, I presume the least we can do is give you a chance."

And so, in the fall of 1986, I began the Nineteenth Annotation of Ignatius of Loyola with the Immaculate Heart of Mary Sisters at a retreat center in Monroe, Michigan. We met together at visitation, a former farm consisting of several small frame houses and a barn which had been converted into a beautiful prayer center. We first got together for an all-day retreat: eight retreatants and five staff persons. I was the only non-Catholic and I think the group was somewhat abashed to discover that they had a Lutheran in their midst. Still, when I asked our priest-participant, who planned to preside at mass for us, if it was okay if I took communion, he looked at me in surprise and asked, "Why ever not?" That was the tone of the whole experience. We were God's children on a journey of faith together: one priest, one woman lay-minister, one parochial schoolteacher (male), one skilled tradesman, another social worker, two housewives, and five nuns.

We learned that the exercises stemmed from Ignatius' own conversion experience, in which he spent thirty days meditating on the life of Jesus, going systematically through the gospels as he did this. He devised a system of contemplation which has become a method of prayer for many subsequent generations of religious inquirers. We were given reading assignments every week, usually from the Bible, but occasionally from Ignatius' own writing. We were instructed in the Ignatian method of prayer: we were to allow our minds to be as open as possible to whatever images or ideas or words might come into them, and to begin to discern those moments when we felt they were coming from God. Ignatius has beautifully articulated criteria for this discernment. The images might relate to the readings or they might not; we were instructed to put ourselves as deeply as possible into the scene or other content of the readings before we began the contemplation. We should try not to "program" what was going to happen.

We were to record the results of our contemplations in a daily journal and my first confusion of this experience with other personal growth experiences came when I later used my journal like a psychological diary. My spiritual director, Sister Mary Lou Theisen, found herself listening to the voice of Sarah rather than the voice of God when I shared my musings with her. "If it does not seem to relate to God's movement in your life, perhaps you don't need to record it," she mildly suggested to me one day.

Mary Lou was a small, gray-haired woman in her late fifties who had been a nun since she was eighteen. After many years of teaching, she accepted a big challenge in her life when she went to India to spend time with Mother Teresa of Calcutta. On returning, she found herself with a conviction that her calling was to be with the poor, and so she became instrumental in developing sheltered housing for the poor elderly in

Mississippi, and then came to visitation to learn how to be a spiritual director.

The role of spiritual director, as the IHM sisters practiced it, was clearly differentiated from that of therapist. The basic question to be asked is, "How is God influencing your life?" rather than, "How can you be well?" And so there is great attention given to the details of daily living. Early in my experience I was encourage to undertake a daily "examen." At the end of each day I was to reflect on the day and try to discern those moments when it seemed that God was somehow present. I have to admit that I rarely did this. My own "biorhythms" are such that discernment is gone by late afternoon, and so most of my commerce with God occurred in the morning hours and was forward-looking rather than retrospective.

In fulfilling my commitment to the "Nineteenth," as we all came to call the exercises, I would take my morning coffee, my Bible, and my journal (a spiral notebook which fell apart by the time eight months had elapsed) and sit quietly in the living room recliner for an hour. Frequently, I could do this before anyone else was awake, but as long as it was accomplished before the rest of the day commenced it seemed to work well for me. At first I tried to be very holy with a candle as an aid to worship, but I discovered that the more mundane and routine the process became, the more integrated into my real life, the more powerfully I experienced what seemed to be God's presence.

I would begin by "centering." Attention to my breathing without using a mantra of any kind seemed to work best for me. After I felt myself to be quiet inside I would invoke God's presence and then would open my Bible to the assigned passage and read it several times. I would then close my eyes and try to picture the scene, if there was a scene, or let whatever words had particularly caught my attention run through my mind a few times. I would then wait as expectantly as I could for whatever appeared in my consciousness. Sometimes I was aware that my own mind was "doing it," but unexpected thoughts and images would frequently float into awareness unbidden, and I would note at a surface level of thought, "Okay. Thanks." I was particularly sensitive to surprises—thoughts and images I wasn't expecting—and to jokes. My experience with what I identify as God is that God frequently catches my attention with thoughts that make me laugh. I was also alert to feelings of intense joy, since that also seemed to be a signal. I would always end with intercessory prayer.

This was not as effortless as that description makes it sound. Frequently, my mind would be so chattery and scattered that even settling down would seem hopeless. Often I was preoccupied with daily concerns which muscled in on the contemplation with annoying power. I devised several strategies for coping with such distractions. The most helpful strategy proved to be the use of my journal for focus. I would give up meditating in my head and do it on paper instead, usually using a dialogue format that Morton Kelsey vividly describes *(Kelsey 1979)*.

Whether I meditated for five minutes or forty minutes (almost never was I able to do it for the prescribed hour), I would then take my journal and quickly record what had occurred. Sometimes the most moving meditations earned only a few sentences and I wondered if in subsequent years I would remember what those were all about. But in the weekly conversations with Mary Lou, I could easily recapitulate the unrecorded content. Her role was to listen quietly (usually I read my journal aloud to her) and to comment on those themes which seemed either puzzling and incongruous or, conversely, affirming. She also called my attention to "graces" which seemed to be occurring, a grace being an unlooked-for gift from God.

I should note parenthetically that I became more and more aware that this kind of deep, content-filled reflection is fraught with hazards if practiced alone and without the input of another person. A basic question which I asked myself at the beginning was how this would differ from free association. There seemed to be several answers to that question. First and most important was the invocation of God's presence. Having practiced a modified version of free association in my personal therapy I can only report my strong impression that the content of my thoughts was very different when I was stringing together impressions and feelings and memories in a therapy session from when I was "watching" images and words appear in contemplation. For one thing, the free association was value-free. What happened, happened. But in contemplation there was an underlying alertness, almost out of awareness, to those images which appeared to be from God and those which appeared to be merely out of my own unconscious or, more ominously, from "the evil one," to use Mary Lou's phrase.

It is part of the genius of the ignatian exercises that after a beautiful introductory series of Bible readings and contemplations on God's love, the first major period of time is spent in meditating deeply, endlessly, boringly, upon sin: our own and the sins of the world. It is as though Ignatius would have us confront the Devil before we become deeply involved with Jesus. (Apparently, Jesus himself underwent the same sequence of experiences when, after his baptism, he spent time in the wilderness.) Week after week we were given contemplation readings on sin, until all of us began to groan "Not again!" In our meeting one week, the group spent a long period of time looking together at photographs of the Holocaust and other horrors of the world. Out of these experiences we were invited to make some sort of commitment to social action in the world. We also were expected to experience a deep repentance for our own sins.

In retrospect it interests me to consider what turned up as the sin that caused my deepest soul to shudder. I found my most powerfully judgmental self. While its unexpected discovery seemed to be a profound grace, many months later I had the terrifying experience of turning that judgmentalism against myself during one long, angry, introspective evening. The Devil had me by the short hairs, and if I ever imagined that my sins were minor and easily outwitted that evening confronted me with their power. Luckily, by then my powers of discernment were more practiced, and when the self-condemnation had exhausted itself I was able to disengage and note what had happened.

It is fascinating to note in my journal that during these times when sin and evil were the dominant themes of the Nineteenth, my personal life was also filled with darkness. Winter was coming on—we began this in November—and my yearly holiday depression reappeared to torment me. Stupid holiday eating resulted in severely bleeding hemorrhoids and I developed a sinus infection which debilitated me for weeks. Purgation at all levels. Mary Lou would merely smile when week after week I dragged my gloomy self to Monroe and reported additional aggravations. I was not depressed in the usual sense, but I was certainly churning up psychological sewage by the bucketful.

And then, mercifully, Christmas came. We began with the Annunciation and day by day became acquainted with Mary and Joseph and the infant. We tried to imagine what his life must have been like. We created images of childhood in our contemplations and connected that long-ago child with our own unique experiences. We found those places in our own childhoods in which God was present for us. For me, it was a rediscovery of family: that large extended biblical family which also included Elizabeth and John the Baptist, and my own large extended family which includes many people with whom I have no blood ties. I tried to remember my own childhood, and I was again the small frightened child who seemed to be inexplicably punished with bad health, and who was baffled by the adult misery which was often present under my family's seemingly serene surface.

During the winter months we journeyed with Jesus through his ministry. I became especially interested in those scripture passages which I found tedious and hard to contemplate. When this occurred, Mary Lou would gently suggest that I spend more time with the verses. Usually, when I would persist I would break through whatever had clogged the flow and there would be a rush of insight. Gradually, Jesus began to become a person for me, even, surprisingly, a person with a face. I have always been amused by evangelical exhortations to "take Jesus into your heart." Somehow Woody Allen's wry facial expression as he announces in one of his movies that he plans to become a Christian pops into my mind. I hear someone saying to him, "You are going to do Jesus Christ?" It is an easy idea to ridicule. The word "God" is nicely vague one prays to "the Ground of Being." But getting to know Jesus?

That turned out to be more wonderful than I would have imagined. "I'm always afraid I made him up," said one of my Monroe friends. When I shared that comment with Mary Lou she noted wonderingly that when she listens to my accounts of Jesus, and then to the accounts of others whom she directs, she is always startled at how much they do, in fact, sound like the same person. And, of course, how they concur with her own experience of Jesus. I can't quite silence my rational mind, but when I need to reply to my skepticism I realize that one of the many things I have learned is that imagination is as "real" as any other form of thought. That we "make up" our existence; our senses are not our only channels in the experience of reality. I'm not at all sure that we don't create reality with our imaginations, maybe in the way that the discoverers of Findhorn created spirits. But that is another subject. I came to cherish those mornings when a vivid presence occupied my meditations and a loving personality seemed to speak to me. It was, after all, the whole point of the Ignatian exercises.

One day in early spring I was meditating on the passage in which two of the disciples ask Jesus where he lives and he replies, "Come and see." (John 1:38-39) 1 had felt stuck—that passage didn't seem to evoke any images for me. Mary Lou told me to repeat it. "Ask Jesus where he lives." So later, without any particular sense that it would get me anywhere, I formed the words in my mind. "Lord, where do you live?" Suddenly, I had an image of myself and Jesus sitting in a cave overlooking a beautiful valley. "Would you like to go down there?" he asked me. Instantly, we were in a field in the valley, near a small village. I had a sense that I was to go into the village, but I felt afraid. "Lord, I'm afraid," I said to Jesus, and as I said it I felt tears start in my eyes. I remember being surprised by the intensity of that feeling, and so I repeated the phrase. "Lord, I'm afraid." Immediately, I was aware that I was standing in the midst of glorious flowers as tall as I was, blowing gently in the wind. "You don't have to go anywhere," Jesus said to me. "You can stay here." I was overwhelmed. It seemed to me to be the most loving thing anyone had ever said to me. I could stay in the field of flowers for as long as I wanted and Jesus would be there with me. I can't remember when I have felt such joy.

During the winter months I stayed at night in the barn, the prayer center which is part of visitation. The small sitting room had a hideaway bed and I was the only guest there during the night. The impact of those nights remains with me still. I expected somehow to feel safe and protected, but instead I was overwhelmed by what I experienced as the energy of the place and I frequently found it hard to sleep. I felt overstimulated and filled with thoughts. It was oddly pleasant, but disquieting.

The Nineteenth Annotation began in October and ended in May. We had a reunion one year later and were interested to discover that no one felt a need to have follow-up meetings, either with the group or with our spiritual directors. The exercises are so carefully constructed that when one is done, one is done.

If I had only one spiritual experience available to me, I would wish it to be the Nineteenth Annotation of Ignatius. Why? First of all, it was extremely compatible with my own personality. I am drawn to "kataphatic prayer"—prayer with content. Also, I like to think on paper, so journaling is a natural outlet. I value the exchange and support of small groups, so the biweekly group meetings were helpful. Indeed, one of the most educational aspects of the experience was listening to our professional religious members—nuns and priest— describe their prayer lives. I had the overwhelming experience of those nights in the barn and the impact of the barn itself, which is such a spiritual power center that it attracts persons from all over southeast Michigan to spend time there in silent reflection and reading (there is a wonderful library) and to attend the gentle, beautiful services.

Whenever I hear someone discount the importance of a physical setting I think of the barn. The thoughtful hospitality of the sisters transforms it into a magical realm of light at Christmas, and into a grotto, complete with a small fountain, at Easter. There are simple statues of ordinary people in unexpected places: in the stairwell, upstairs on the balcony, by the front door. There is the wonderful smell of always burning candles, and the soft rustle of feet coming and going and chairs being quietly moved, but no other sounds. The crucifix is merely two sticks fastened together hanging on the rough wooden wall, and there is a simple medieval icon painting of a madonna and child on the opposite wall; mysteriously and wonderfully I was to encounter the same icon as a focus of meditation when I went to Shalem. There are rocking chairs and floor cushions to rest on. The whole barn opens its arms in modesty, in comfort, in peace. The doors are unlocked at seven in the morning and not locked again until evening. People are free to come without notice and to use the facility quietly for their own purposes. When the Sisters put out a registry book at the entrance they were astonished to see how many people were using the place. Until that time they had had no way of knowing.

When I finished the Ignatian exercises I seriously considered joining the Catholic Church. Unfortunately, subsequent experience convinced me (sadly) that the world of Catholicism is too distant from the world to which God has assigned me, and would be too alienating from my family and close friends. But the Catholics remain for me cherished and exotic friends whom I think of with great tenderness and gratitude.

CHAPTER 9

Encountering The Holy Spirit

Spiritual direction can be defined as "sensitivity to the Holy Spirit." That was news to me. For years I thought I was supposed to pray to God-the-Creator ("Our Father who art in Heaven . . .") and I pictured God as "out there," separate from myself. But the God-voice inside—myself as "God-imprinted"—gradually became more recognizable as I experienced it in more and more places. I don't know if the Ignatian Exercises came before or after the encounters I want to talk about now, but the cumulative effect was a heightened awareness of the many ways I could be open to God's voice, and Pendle Hill, Shalem, and Kansas are now merged in my memory.

PENDLE HILL

I had first encountered the Quakers at Earlham College, a Quaker school. When our son Jeff was a student there we attended worship meetings in the typically plain meetinghouse on the edge of the campus. It was what the Quakers call "a programmed meeting," meaning there was singing and a sermon, and we were impressed by its simplicity and sweetness. Later I began attending the "unprogrammed meeting" in Ann Arbor, consisting of an hour of silence with occasional spontaneous sharings of insights, and I was a regular attender there for about two years. I seriously considered joining the Society of Friends, as the Quakers call themselves, but was somewhat put off by some aspects of their theology (God the

Father and God the Son often seem to be discounted) and by the absence of music in the unprogrammed meetings.

Out of what I think of as my Quaker years came an ongoing subscription to the *Friends Journal*, a Quaker magazine. In that beautiful little publication I began reading about a place called Pendle Hill in Wallingford, Pennsylvania, near Philadelphia. It became clear to me that Pendle Hill was central to Quaker life in this country, and so, when our son Bruce moved to Philadelphia, it occurred to me that I might have a chance to visit Pendle Hill. I wrote to them for information and learned that Pendle Hill is a study center with semester or yearlong programs for those who wish to become regular students. However, they also offer a category they call "sojourner," meaning someone who visits for a week only but is free to attend classes and otherwise enter into the life of the community. That sounded perfect for me.

I went to Pendle Hill as a sojourner in November 1986. I discovered that it resembles a shabby, very small college campus on wooded grounds adjacent to Swarthmore College, also a Quaker institution. When I first walked into the little stone house which was identified as the main building, no one was around except the cooks, so I hesitantly went into the kitchen and identified myself as a new sojourner. A friendly young woman interrupted her bread making in order to undertake a couple of phone calls on my behalf, and after a few moments a second woman who was to be in charge of my arrangements appeared with another sojourner in tow, a young man with cerebral palsy whom she had been showing around the grounds. That week we were the only sojourners.

I was taken to my room upstairs in the rustic building which also housed the worship facility, the "meeting room," directly below my room. The building reminded me of summer camp lodges I have known. It was very old and drafty, but I discovered that I had been given the only private bathroom, so that was a real luxury. (Because I developed flu that week, I was grateful for the bathroom.) My room had an amusing feature: a hole in the floor through which I could see and hear anything going on in the meeting room. There also was a note on my bathroom door asking me not to flush the toilet during meeting times.

I was given a program of ongoing classes and activities—meetings, lectures, art activities, and workdays—and invited to sign up for whatever interested me. I chose to attend a class on the mystic tradition in Islam, a class on the meaning of spirituality, and a daily pottery workshop. Every morning there was a meeting for worship. Each Wednesday was devoted to work on the grounds and buildings; people were given the opportunity to sign up for work at the level appropriate to their strength, so I dragged my flu-ridden body to the library where I helped to catalog books.

I think of my week at Pendle Hill as "spacious" in a peculiarly nice way. The residents were warm, friendly, and interested, but non-intrusive. At mealtimes about thirty people were regularly present and the food was an important part of the experience: delicious whole wheat bread, fresh peanut butter, and jugs of homemade apple butter at every meal, a table of specially prepared food for the vegetarians, and lots of fresh vegetables, seeds, and grains to supplement whatever the main course proved to be. Rarely desserts—I was reminded of the Frances LaLappe's *Diet For a Small Planet* books.

Even short-term guests like myself were quickly incorporated into the regular conversations at meals and I noticed that nearly every day there were visitors of various descriptions from unusual places. For example, one day we housed and fed a contingent from a peace march which had recently made its way across the country; at our table that night we had two young women and several school-age children who had been on the march for three months. It was fascinating to talk with the poised, intelligent children for whom this was surely the experience of a lifetime. The pacifism and social activism of the Quakers was vibrant and ubiquitous at Pendle Hill, a central meeting place and home base. The energy generated by the many ongoing projects was impressive, but even more impressive were the good will and lack of anger which char-acterize Quaker activities. I had an uncomfortable sense of my own sloth and cowardice as I listened to accounts of personal commitments on the part of those with whom I talked every day.

In what ways were psychological and spiritual concerns simultaneously addressed at Pendle Hill? The two were never separated. No religious group I have ever encountered so seamlessly lives out their personal psychology through their spirituality. Pendle Hill is an educational center for spiritual seekers and a refuge for lost souls. One woman, whose husband had recently died, told me that after she and he had come as sojourners ten years earlier, she comforted herself with the thought that no matter what happened in her life, no matter how hard it was, "I can always go back to Pendle Hill." And so she had come back as a regular student and experienced, as she expected to do, not only the gentle support of the community, but nourishment for her mind and spirit.

What do I retain from my week with the Quakers? I am aware of an internal smile as I remember it. In spite of my recalcitrant health (and in spite of a week of cold rain! I had to trek to a nearby town to buy some warmer clothes and an umbrella) I remember especially the sense of freedom. Because I was there for one week only I remained a somewhat anonymous visitor, and as such I experienced an appealing combination of friendliness and reserve. It was as if I finally had the chance to be somewhat invisible at the same time I was safe and cared for—it is hard to describe. There is a "Quaker courtesy" which I first ran into at Earlham and experienced anew at Pendle Hill: a combination of politeness and kindness that I find irresistible.

Of course, I remember the classes with great pleasure. I learned about the mystical tradition in the "Quran." I listened to thoughtful discussions of spiritual "leadings" in the Quaker tradition. Above all I remember the afternoons in the quiet clay studio because out of that experience came my avocation as a clay sculptor, a serendipity I never could have foreseen.

There is a magic at Pendle Hill which is, I feel sure, directly related to its theology. Central to Quaker beliefs is the idea of "that of God in every person." George Fox, its founder, taught that if one related to that of God in another, not only did one experience one's own "inner light," but also somehow fanned the flame in the other person. I have a vivid memory of an elderly Quaker softly remonstrating an agitated, angry speaker during one of our local Friends' meetings with the phrase, "That is not the Friendly way." In my own inner life there remain many Quaker phrases and ideas: "That speaks to my condition." "Speak truth to strength." "Look for the opening," and (a phrase my teenage children became sick of) "A way will open." Also, "Mind the light," and the idea of not cloaking the child of God, who is oneself, in the trappings of hierarchy, including titles, last names, and pretentious clothes.

While I was at Pendle Hill there was much concern over the decaying buildings and inadequate space. Even though everyone seemed to be aware of the problems, there was serious reluctance to tamper with the place. There was a fear that they might somehow destroy the magic if they modernized. I don't know what has happened in the years since I was there but I somehow doubt that the magic has to do with the physical facilities—or not, at least, with them primarily.

I was interested to learn that there was an ongoing connection between the Quakers and the founders of the Visitation Barn. Local Quakers were regularly been drawn to the barn for contemplation, and Sister Ann, an IHM Sister in her mid-eighties, had been consulting with the Quakers about setting up "houses of prayer" on the barn model. It is a lovely idea.

Just as I was tempted to join the Catholics after my experience in Monroe, so I have been ongoingly tempted to join the Quakers. But as was true of Catholicism, Quakerism is very much a foreign country requiring a level of commitment I'm ashamed to admit I am not prepared to give. The Quakers have no clergy and this means that everyone must assume responsibility for the ongoing success of the meeting. Also, the branch of Quakerism I am drawn to does not have music as part of the worship, and I miss music dreadfully. But I hold the Quakers in my heart as models of the possible and I too am comforted to know that, should I ever need to go there, Pendle Hill would be there to take me in.

KANSAS

On a hot, dry summer evening in 1985, I carried my bags across the broken sidewalk of the Manna House of Prayer, on a dusty, rundown side street on the wrong side of the tracks in the village of Concordia, Kansas, past weeds and a struggling patch of grass, into the old, shabby frame building. The trip from Illinois had taken longer than I had anticipated and I was late. I smelled dinner as I heard a cheery voice call out, "Are you Sarah? We were worried about you." It was Sister Julia Norton, who in any other setting would have looked like an unusually weary Junior Leaguer; tall, thin, intense, wearing a neat cotton dress, with her legs bare and her sandals worn. She led me into the big cool seminar room where the group had already gathered.

We were twenty-four participants and five staff members, of all ages and from all kinds of denominations and societal backgrounds, and from as far away as Maine. The building was an ancient former hospital with black and white tile floors conspicuously laid out in a swastika design; before the Nazi corrupted it the swastika was a kind of cross. There was air-conditioning on alternate floors to save money, and when there were not retreats in session the Sisters of St. Joseph, who operated the center, turned it off. Each of us had a bare private room; clean, absolutely quiet, serene. The food was cooked by the Sisters and was plain, much of it homegrown, and perfectly delicious.

We began work at nine each morning, worked as a group until noon, and then in the afternoons we participated in individual guided imagery sessions called "travels," either as "travelers" or "guides" or observers. Each "journey" took at least two hours and most of us had at least one session lasting close to three hours. Every participant traveled at least five times during the two weeks, and acted as guide at least once. We reconvened as a group every evening and worked for three more hours. (The two weeks were not called "intensive" without reason.)

My journal details the daily events and so, in order to recapture my depth of experience, I am selecting two passages that seem to me to summarize the essence of our activities. I will not attempt to analyze the symbols or background history, except as I find it already in the journal, but others may freely interpret.

July 31, 1985—Every minute of our time is filled. In the mornings we have lectures and group exercises. In the afternoons one either travels or observes someone else. The heavy work is one-to-one; someone acts as guide and most of the time there is an observer in the room also. I would have thought that would inhibit the process, but was assured that one quickly forgets about the presence of the observer. I can see that the observer has a valuable function, not only for learning but as an objective presence in a time of intense personal encounter.

We are legitimizing the mystical content that was always present in the Gestalt work but never acknowledged. Whereas Gestalt work took place in a "meaningless" life-field and did not (technically) allow for spiritual input, here we assume that we are surrounded by the Higher Unconscious and that, just as repressed material strains to pop into consciousness from "below," so also repressed yearnings and "gifts" strain to pop into consciousness from "above." Somehow it is hard to talk about this without conceptual maps—we are constantly being reminded that "the map is not the territory."

The theoretical material is from Roberto Assagioli's psychology—psychosynthesis—which I had always equated with such stuff as Scientology and the Rosecrucians. It dates back to the middle part of the century and Assagioli's association with Jung, who is hiding in every corner around here. There is a lot of material on symbols, images, complexes, archetypes, subpersonalities, dreams, and so forth: all of the ways in which the ineffable expresses itself in our consciousness. It seems terribly familiar, except that we don't ordinarily see these symbols and experiences as pathways to personal growth.

There are some general symbols which we all use as vehicles, or canvasses, or frames within which to do our "imaging." A meadow stands for consciousness itself, light is God, a "wisdom figure" is our inner spirit, which can be Jesus, but not necessarily. (Fritz Perls turned up for me yesterday; do you believe that wicked old man guiding me around my fantasy?) A forest stands for the subconscious, and so forth.

The "work" is done lying down. "You will stay in your consciousness if you sit up," my guide told me. Basically, it is free association fantasy—guided imagery—"one goes where one is led." The guide nudges occasionally or makes sure the wisdom figure is there to help, and in some sense one is in a trance state. I kept laughing at Fritz Perls because he was so funny and so outrageous—he wouldn't let me get pompous or holy, but he was indeed very helpful. Mysterious!!

I need to record my first journey. A new friend, who is also a guide and staff person, feels that this is important, even though one feels that one will never forget what happened!

One always begins in the meadow. One quickly learns that these personal meadows vary drastically from person to person and from time to time. Yesterday there was a tiny little mineshaft in the middle of my meadow, and Fritz got us shovels and we dug down until we created a lovely pond into which I promptly went swimming. Later I journeyed through my Forest and Lo! I came out at the "This is the Place" park overlooking Salt Lake City. All kinds of stuff was going on in the valley, and I was invited to come down and homestead, but I realized I couldn't—it was very painful—instead Fritz and I sat up on the mesa and watched. I asked Fritz what I was supposed to do and he just grinned wickedly and said, "Don't do anything. People will come to you." That seemed exactly right, and I was aware of being bathed in *intense* white light, which was both extremely pleasant and *blinding*. (I hesitate to write this down, it sounds so melodramatic, but my inner voice this morning told me to write down everything.) Then it gradually faded and I left the fantasy exhausted, but feeling satisfied that I had done what I was supposed to do.

Of course, in the two hours a lot of small episodes occurred in the fantasy; for example, my mother turned up in the form of a small deer; surprised me quite considerably.

In the evening we (the entire group) again worked with symbols—we found a comfortable place on the floor, the lights were dimmed, and in response to the direction to "image" whatever we thought we were supposed to be, I had a sudden vision of myself as a Buddha sitting under a Banyan tree—I seemed to be both the Buddha and the tree. Two such sedentary images!—sitting on the Salt Lake Bench, and sitting under a Banyan tree. Reminds me of my Jonah symbol (note: this is from prior work), only I trust God will not cause my tree to shrivel up the way Jonah's did. Oddly (only nothing seems very odd around here), my guide made an impulsive reference to Jonah, and then looked surprised and said, "Well, I don't know where that came from. I never make Old Testament references."

August 3—In our work tonight we were invited to go from our meadow into a "prayer garden" where we would find a "vase" and a "sword" (not very subtle symbols!) I found myself in a stubbly field where I immediately saw a white unicorn the size of a horse— it seemed important. It was restlessly and elegantly wandering around. A grove of trees was between me and the Salt Lake Valley (again.) When I went into the prayer garden, it looked like the "Mother House" of the Sisters, which we had just visited yesterday, but I willfully turned it into an azalea garden with a lovely pond, which was much nicer. The unicorn came in too. The vase was a chalice. The sword was thin and silver and sharp. The unicorn said his name was "Gift," which I thought was a dumb name, but he wouldn't change it. *(Taggart journal 1985)*

The sexual symbolism was, of course, intended, and it is difficult in these few pages to capture the depth and richness of the images with which we continually worked. Not only did we call our own higher and lower treasures into consciousness, we continually shared in the treasures of others. One had the sense of spending two weeks with the brothers Grimm. Bruno Bettleheim was exactly right in considering the uses of enchantment (Bettleheim 1975) the ways in which legends and fairy tales capture universal themes. We even, one night, spent several hours with hundreds of art postcards, so that we communed with the great artists of the world and experienced their visual representations of the Collective Unconscious.

Group experiences of any kind, in which intimacy is fostered and trust engendered through mutual sharing, tend in my experience to be healing and love-promoting occasions. But in this sanctified setting, with a Christian liturgy twice a week and ubiquitous presence of the faith of the participants, there was acceptance and gentle affirmation at a level I had not experienced elsewhere. If I had no other reason to feel that the process was useful and profound, the memory of loving friendships and the growth I observed in even the most fragile and defensive of the participants would persuade me.

In 1988 I returned to Kansas to participate in a second Spiritual Guidance Intensive. It was the only one of my explorations which I repeated. I was reassured to discover that my inner world had changed and that in some sense I had moved on. The process proved to be as enlightening and growthful as it had been previously, and it seemed to write an appropriate finis to my pilgrimage. Several years later, however, after yet another workshop in Detroit, I became better acquainted with Harold Edwards himself, and at that time I offered to help him turn his wonderful process into a book, which we eventually called *Pearl Diving, a Psychosynthesis Approach to Spiritual Direction*, and which is now searching for a publisher.

SHALEM

Early in my explorations a friend had urged me to search out books by the psychiatrist Gerald May. When I finally obtained a copy of his book, *Will and Spirit*, I felt a sense of envious dismay. Here between the covers of a single book were many of the ideas that I myself had laboriously been trying to develop. I read it and reread it. Here was mystical experience taken seriously by a professional psychiatrist. Here was an elegant phenomenology and psychology of mysticism. Here was practical advice on how to incorporate respect for mystical experience into psychological practice, plus caveats about the differences between the two. My reactions were much the same as when I first read Scott Peck's *The Road Less Traveled*. In some sense it felt like "my book." What was left to be said?

I noticed that Gerald May had been a cofounder of a training center for spiritual formation called Shalem (pronounced "Shalaim") in Washington, D.C. I wrote to the address on the dust jacket of the book and was astonished to receive a prompt, hand-written reply from "Jerry" urging me to phone him to identify the appropriate time and format for a visit. When I did so he recommended that I attend a workshop called "Spiritual Guidance for Spiritual Guides," which was aimed at persons already working with some sort of spiritual direction, whether or not that was what they called it.

So in February 1987, I drove to the Sisters of Bon Secour Retreat Center in horse-farm country near Baltimore for a five-day retreat. I was one of twenty-five participants who met together that first evening in a large, somewhat formal circle in the attractive living room-meeting room of the center with the three directors of Shalem: Dr. May, Episcopal priest Tilden Edwards, and Catholic Sister Rosemary Daugherty. The group consisted primarily of clergy and about equally of men and women, a bit unusual because most women clergy of that historical time were recently ordained and usually did not have time for this sort of personal enrichment. Most participants appeared to be over fifty. There were a number of retired laypersons, including, interestingly, a retired CIA officer who was wrestling with the collective sins of the world. The group was more upper-middle-class than I had found in other workshops of this kind, with a sort of "Ivy League" quality: intellectual, polite, from (I would guess) moneyed families and "good schools." Predominantly Episcopalian (Shalem comes out of an Episcopal background and was originally based at the Washington Cathedral), although there was one Church of God pastor, several Presbyterians, and several Roman Catholic nuns. It was a group that sat in chairs, not on the floor—at first, at least.

I came expecting to learn how to do spiritual guidance, and found instead that most of the four days were spent in various kinds of spiritual exercises—especially in prayer and meditation. The premise at Shalem is that someone mature in the faith helps an inquirer to discern God's activity in his or her life, and that one comes to such a "conversation" on both sides "in prayer." There is no "technique" to spiritual guidance, but rather an acquired ability to listen to the Holy Spirit at the same time one is listening to another person. One starts from the faith position that if one listens, God will speak. In fact, several of the four days were spent in silence, broken only by occasional periods of processing.

Those days of silence were, indeed, revelational for me. I was drawn to an anguished cruciform in the chapel where I spent much of my time in contemplation of suffering, and I also spent time in my tiny little individual room which contained a rocking chair in addition to the usual bed, desk, and bureau. It was a particularly pleasant room in which to meditate, and when, on the second day, a late winter blizzard snowed us in, the sense of isolation and silence became profound.

Cofounder Tilden Edwards, an ascetic-looking priest with a face straight off a medieval icon, has written movingly of the results of this sort of meditation. I know now, though I did not at the time, that this is a singularly Christian-Buddhist description, and reflects the influence of Buddhist thought on many Christian spiritual leaders, including Jerry May and Jack Biersdorf. Tilden writes:

> Meister Eckhart said, "God does not ask anything of you except that you let yourself go and let God be God in you." If we could really do that, what else could God ask? But just what does it

mean to "let yourself go and let God be God in you"? We each have our own way of groping for an answer. At this point in my own groping, it means to let go, as empowering grace is given, of our ultimate identity with the little self made up of our confused, fearful and willful grasping and accumulating; to let go of our primary identity with this isolating, possessive sense of self. As the hardness of this identity softens, our true self in God, our spiritual heart, is gradually strengthened as the place of our real identity. This deep self lives in free coalescence with God, moment by moment. It is a unique personal transparency through which God's Spirit radiates; cleansing, refreshing, loving, discerning, creating . . . What most clearly is in our power is a capacity to pray for it. God seems to mysteriously respect and wait upon our expressed willingness to accept the ever-present invitation. A second way we can assist is by periods of becoming still inside, willing to wait upon God through the little self's speed, fear, greed, and cultivated attachments, willing in God's good time to drop through these to our real Home in God with its liberating sufficiency and suffusion in Love . . . . May each of us participate in this holy Way, letting go and letting God be God in us. (*Edwards, 1986, in press*)

During the course of every year, Shalem offers a carefully disciplined program of spiritual formation through the use of intentional small groups, and also offers training to spiritual directors through a three-year instructional program in spiritual guidance. One can participate locally in a Washington-based format, or nationally as an off-campus student with occasional weekends or weeks in the Washington area.

I was impressed with the professional seriousness of Shalem; "professional" in the sense of competent, ethical, and well-informed, with clearly defined boundaries and purpose. I was also impressed with the gentle, self-effacing staff, people for whom fame and success seemed to be of very little concern. And above all I was impressed with the wealth of knowledge, experience, and intellectual rigor which underlay the whole enterprise.

What did I learn during the week at Shalem? I learned some impressive things about prayer. I learned (again) that when I manage to keep my internal mouth shut, I seem to experience an interior voice of wisdom and love. I learned about the power of imagery: the cruciform encapsulated my own experience with suffering and thrust me into a sharp center of pain which remained undissolved. The icon of the mother and child became my mother, my child, my grandchild. I experienced vivid and surprising dreams which enriched and stimulated my prayer experience, the more so because I could not talk about them. Once in the middle of the night I awoke from one of the saddest dreams I have ever had and wept for a long while. I was drawn to reading and (especially) to writing; nothing new for me.

The periods of silence warped my usual sense of time, so that I found myself going to bed at sunset and waking on a monk's schedule at 3:00 in the morning. There was deep pleasure in the brief connection with wise, good people—both staff and participants—and with the beauty of the setting (and the wonderful homey food!).

I remember the Shalem experience with deep gratitude, but because spiritual guidance did not turn out to be my future vocation, and because I had become impressed with Harold Edwards' psychosynthesis method of spiritual direction, the week in that snowy Baltimore retreat center remains a serene and impressive detour. However, a decade later I realize that the awareness of "no-self" I have alluded to in this account first occurred in recognizable form at Shalem—an awareness that becomes increasingly powerful as I near my journey's end.

10

Paved with Good Intentions

When I was young I was taught that good and evil are relative and that what is called "evil" is the result of environmental deprivation of some kind. As I have already noted, the concept of sin had no place in my family's life. Sin was belittled as a destructive source of unnecessary guilt. But life experience eventually caused me to wonder if psychological explanations are always true. Over the years I found myself particularly disturbed by pride—hubris, as the Greeks called it—because it so often masquerades as self-confidence. I first encountered professional hubris during my TB years: a holier-than-thou attitude that I later experienced also in university settings, both as student and teacher. But a peculiar sort of hubris came into focus for me in the summer of 1986, when I spent sixteen days at the Guild for Psychological Studies, a Jungian center at Four Springs, in the hills above California's Napa Valley.

I had been warned that people sometimes found Four Springs aversively rigid, but I had no idea before I went there how powerfully upset I would be by the experience. Afterward, when I described this reaction to a friend, she shivered and said she wondered if I had had a sense of evil while I was there. It was the first time anyone had used that label and the word struck me as exactly correct. I began to wonder if evil was sometimes subtly present in otherwise benign situations, something that also seemed to be happening years later in my Lutheran church home. After the summer was over I decided to try to identify the specific events that caused my distress, and to examine as honestly as I could those inner "shadows" (to use the Jungian term) that I might have been projecting onto the experience. I wanted to see if I could distinguish projections from objective reality.

Four Springs consists of three hundred gorgeous acres up a long, steep country road. One has the sense of being a million miles from civilization, except that on quiet days, highway noises can faintly be heard. All kinds of terrain present themselves: deep woods, meadow, orchards (at Four Springs they preserved their own plums, pears, and applesauce, and in summer have berries and figs), and, as the name suggests, four springs which feed a little stream and pool. Burbling water can be heard in many places—I was told that by late summer the water would dry up but I was there in June. The physical facility consists of a log cabin-style lodge, many small cabins sprinkled here and there among the trees, a small library, a new seminar cabin with a big stone fireplace, a tiny meditation building overlooking the hills, and (gesture to the hot summers) a big swimming pool. The "facilities" were in a small bathhouse, with plenty of hot water but otherwise no heat.

I found life at Four Springs to be an odd combination of camping and resort. It was very cold the first week I was there, and as I had not brought winter clothes I had to engage in creative layering, which meant that my blue jeans and two wool sweaters got heavy use. We set the tables for twenty at most meals and all work except the actual cooking was done cooperatively by everyone. We were only twelve actual participants that session and ours was an interesting group with ages ranging from the mid-thirties to late seventies, heavy on social workers and clergy. Two of the nicest men were gay (not a couple). It was a comfortable environment for diversity.

But what shocked me soon after I got there—what I could not have anticipated—was Four Springs' aggressive objection to Christianity as an organized religion. Indeed, "Christianity" turned out to be a dirty word at Four Springs. If they had advertised themselves as an ecumenical center I would have been less upset (I notice that recent brochures have been revised to include that information), but at that time there was no advanced warning. The cheap shots at the church (any church) were relentless and especially got under my skin because we spent three hours every morning (and I mean every morning, including Saturdays and Sundays) studying "The Basic Records of Jesus' Life," which means literally what it says. It soon became clear that the purpose of the seminar was to return to the so-called "authentic message" of the human person, Jesus of Nazareth. This was not purely demythologizing (they respected myths) but rather "de-churchifying."

At Four Springs they taught that Jesus did not identify himself as the Messiah, but rather sought to reveal a "kingdom of God" in each person's present life. They stressed that God's special presence in Jesus' life was, by extension, potentially available in each of our lives. Elizabeth Howes, the founder of Four Springs, had a Jungian and (I must admit) moving concept of the All-Inclusive-God, but it was a concept very much at odds with traditional understanding. God, she believed, has both light and shadow sides. God is Wounder, Wounded, Wound, and Healer. God suffers. God needs our help in creation. God sometimes sleeps, needs to be importuned, and expects us to make hard choices. It was in many ways an interesting theology, but it disturbed me that it was not identified as theology, but rather was considered to be "truth." Several times I suggested the word "theology" to staff members and was met with blank stares. These were people steeped in the idea of scientific psychology and they were offering us psychological knowledge—Jungian knowledge—which would, it was alleged, liberate us from the superstition offered to us by the traditional church.

The Jungian aspect of the experience came, among other ways, in the ubiquitous availability of therapy. The staff was available for informal talks at most any time—frequently, in my case, initiated by them, since early on I was apparently identified as a dissenter. But several participants also started what they intended to be ongoing individual therapy with staff members. The staff people were not paid, but because they were almost all therapists, many from the San Francisco area, they derived an ongoing clientele from the program, a coincidence I undiplomatically noted on my last day there.

One of the most disquieting aspects of Four Springs was the emphasis on secrecy. I am accustomed to the therapeutic norm of "confidentiality," but this was more than that—this was a subtle atmosphere of hiddenness. Elizabeth Howes was suspicious of group therapy ("we are individuals in a group") and personal privacy was alleged to be assiduously maintained, though participants apparently were discussed in staff meetings, so "privacy" existed primarily between those of us who were not staff. We were never asked to share personal experiences or feelings except in individual therapy sessions, so our classes together had an odd aspect of superficiality. Though I liked the staff very much—they seemed humane, straightforward, and competent—I had only been there a short time when I got an uncomfortable feeling of social control. In spite of the lip service paid to collegiality and individual responsibility, the place began to seem hierarchical and subtly authoritarian.

However (to be fair), for many people Four Springs had, over the years, become a compelling and integrative way of life. Indeed, a kind of "cult" apparently developed, albeit a supportive and loving one. Many people attended the Basic Records over and over again, and there were also other seminars throughout the year, as well as work-weekends for caretaking the property. Perhaps, I thought to myself, if people were looking for community and meaning, but couldn't quite handle church, this was a nice substitute. The acceptance of all kinds of lifestyles and backgrounds was impressive, as were the simplicity and gracefulness of daily life. Furthermore, the administrators evidently had worked hard to keep the cost down, so much so that I wondered how they managed to pay the bills. But a decade later, in an era of proliferating cults, I look back at Four Springs and recognize the model.

Typical of the Four Springs economical use of time was a prompt lunch on the first day, after which we adjourned to the seminar room and began our first class. Even on "day zero," as they called it, no time was wasted. The seminar building was a single large room with a big stone fireplace in the corner and Windsor chairs placed in a tidy circle around the periphery. In front of each chair was a footstool—a small, cloth-covered box topped with a cushion—which created an atmosphere of almost oriental serious-ness, reinforced when we were told to leave our shoes outside; it was the custom never to wear shoes in the seminar room. In the center of the room were two Navajo rugs; accepted icons at Four Springs were frequently American Indian. The two tall candles on ceremonial ledges above the fireplace were solemnly lit by the leaders before each seminar session commenced.

In 1986, when I was there, Four Springs had been operating in its present location for thirty-five years and many customs had evolved over that period of time. For example, participants and staff were referred to by their full names, so that I was "Sarah Taggart" (as if my name had a hyphen); it made me think of name references in Russian novels. All activities were announced by a gong, sounded slowly enough so that between the first sounding and the last people had time to regroup and change location. Much of the non-programmed day was spent in mandatory silence, and the stern warning to bring no radios was taken so seriously that even during the first days of the Chernobyl nuclear accident we were dependent on the cook's car radio to reassure us that the world would survive; there were no other available resources except an afternoon newspaper which was brought into the lodge before dinner.

The rarely varying days began at 6:15, or as a special treat if there had been an evening party or some other tiring event, at 6:30. Saturdays and Sundays were treated very much like weekdays in that there was a full schedule of classes on both days. At 6:45 there was a morning ceremony with music and "movement" (any kind of free, dancelike movement, done in my case with my eyes tightly closed so I could think, childlike, that others couldn't watch me making a fool of myself) as well as a reading appropriate to the day's study topics. Then breakfast was eaten in silence at 7:00. The silence was broken at 8:30 when the morning seminar began.

Every morning after breakfast the staff had a meeting. It soon became clear that, among other purposes, these meetings were what in another setting would have been called case conferences, and that I soon became one of the cases. Memories of having been subject to case conferences during the years of my tuberculosis— my life totally in the hands of others—contributed to my subsequent feelings of discomfort. I had not agreed to become a "case," but I seemed to have no choice in the matter because we were never consulted nor informed that we were being discussed. I surmised that I was a case when I was singled out by various staff members for what seemed to be therapeutic interviews. I felt myself to be back in the helpless position of "patient" and this was reinforced by the helplessness created by the isolated setting without telephones or cars. (I have since wondered if we were thought of as students. No, the assumptions were much more clinical than they were educational.)

On the afternoon of Day One, we were invited to paint Jesus' baptism in any way it came to us to do so. We were furnished with tempera paints, brushes, and newsprint. When we had finished, we displayed our work in the seminar room and, without identifying who painted what, we discussed our impressions. In vivid primary colors we had portrayed implosions and explosions and transformations. Here, for the first time, the specifically Jungian approach to this study became apparent. Through this nonverbal activity we had bypassed those intellectualizations through which we were believed to hide from ourselves, and through vicariously participating in Jesus' baptism we were ourselves in some sense baptized. We brought into conscious awareness whatever primal baptismal experience lay hidden in our own unconscious. Jesus' life modeled the universal human drama for us in a sort of one-of-a-kind metaphor, so that, as the pictures painted themselves onto each of our papers, out of our own unconscious psyches seemed to come those truths which were both universal and uniquely ours, our own contributions to the ongoing evolution of the collective unconscious, as Jungian psychology would put it.

Someone whispered to me, "Ontogeny recapitulates phylogeny," as we were leaving the seminar room on that first day, and I was startled because I had made the same connection. Somehow the Jungian idea of the collective unconscious implies that inside each of us is a recapitulation of the psychological history of the human race. In a way we are psychological holograms. So each day we were to take the scripture lessons into our private time, and out of our unconscious reserves to create our own versions of the events studied in the morning lesson. We painted, wrote in our journals, held small group discussions, created mimes, sculpted—there was a rich variety of possibilities.

There were a number of ceremonial occasions. On Friday nights someone lit the "Shabbat candles." On Sundays the routine was slightly varied by having religious music played during breakfast—classical music with some sort of religious motif. Also on Sunday there was a bread and wine ceremony in the meditation room; one by one we were invited to remove our shoes and go into the room alone to partake of the bread and wine we would find inside in any way which was comfortable for us to do. For myself, there was something strangely distasteful in this solitary "communion."

There were also several ceremonies in the "hogan," a large circular area of mowed grass with strategically placed rocks at the entrance and elsewhere which one was encouraged to touch reverently as one entered and left the circle. The movement around the hogan circle was always clockwise; this was deemed important by the Navajos, whose ceremony we were repeating. I found this the one ceremony in which I was stubbornly unwilling to take part; biblical admonitions against idolatry kept occurring to me, even though I knew at a rational level that this sort of innocent observation is only play-acting.

Also Indian was a ceremony in which we got up before sunrise and walked up a steep trail to an overlook where we could then see the sun rise. We did a "dance" to help the sun come up. It was very cold and we were not entirely reverent when we discovered ourselves having to wait many weary moments before our efforts were finally rewarded. I enhanced the Indian ambience by wrapping myself in a blanket to keep warm.

Let me describe our studies, because they were central to my eventual distress. We used a text by Professor Henry Burton Sharman called *The Records of Jesus' Life* (1915). Disillusionment by Albert Schweitzer and others with the possibility of discovering the historical Jesus had apparently not impressed the founders of Four Springs. (In recent years the so-called "Jesus Seminar" has continued this futile endeavor—the modern world attempting to discredit God, so to speak.)

The method of study itself was exemplary; in general I was much impressed by it and wished I had used it when I myself was teaching. We employed what our leaders referred to as "the empty bowl." That is, we were to imagine that in the middle of the room was a huge empty bowl which we would fill with our ideas. The bowl would hold all ideas indiscriminately, and questions raised were understood to have no right or wrong answers. When a topic seemed to elicit no more ideas we would move on to another question. Theoretically, it was assumed that this method would allow for a completely open discussion, free from preconceptions. In practice, it was my observation that the leaders, through selective questioning, led us to "discover" for ourselves their subtle and undisclosed theology. Their questions frequently had implied "correct" answers. And even more troubling to me was the fact that the scripture readings themselves eliminated gospel passages, including many of the most familiar ones, that contradicted the Four Springs theology.

This theology was concerned with four universal themes or "archetypes," in Jungian terminology: Virgin Birth, Death and Rebirth, Wounded Healer, and Savior. Of course, traditional Pauline theology is based on these themes, and the Four Springs people contrasted Paul's archetypal ideas to the actual teachings of the human Jesus. Freeing ourselves from Paul's ideas would, presumably, free our psyches from superstitious mythologies and allow us to experience God as Jesus had experienced God.

Jesus was held up as the depth psychologist who foresaw our modern understanding of the human unconscious. It was believed that Jesus engaged in a brief and intense ministry in which he taught that by knowing and understanding our inner selves ("The Kingdom of God is within you") we could be transformed by the same Spirit that had transformed him, and through not resisting evil, but using our self-awareness in loving ways, we could participate in the Kingdom of Heaven right here on earth.

References to evil, and to such things as separating sheep from goats and wheat from chaff, were believed to be editorial additions by the authors of the gospels, and the genuine, historical Jesus did not have a dualistic concept of evil, but rather understood that God has a "shadow" side, and that one cannot understand reality except as a unified whole. Thus, we are adjured to be "whole," meaning to be aware of and in control of our own shadow selves. What we have traditionally called evil is nothing more than the projection of our unidentified collective shadow selves, and acknowledging and experiencing all aspects of ourselves is the only way to solve the problem of evil in the world.

It is a compelling theology if one doesn't examine it too closely, but it is very much at odds with traditional Christian beliefs—the "overlay of St. Paul" as the Four Springs people sarcastically put it—and superstitious "resurrection" accounts were dismissed out of hand. In particular, theirs was a theology that rejected so-called dualism, and dualism, as I will discuss in the next chapter, seems to me to be central to an understanding of evil.

Four Springs founder Elizabeth Howes then nearly eighty, was an archetypal figure: ancient, gaunt, and unspeakably wise. Her fierce eyes blazed out of a large bony face, and the passion of her words was lit up by her humor. She seemed to concentrate totally on whomever she was talking with, and this was reinforced by her seemingly total recall for names. There was an androgynous quality about her—she was big-boned and forthright—but in contrast to her somewhat masculine appearance, I particularly remember her in a floor-length dress of brightly colored, hand-woven fabric—such a feminine costume. She had recently broken a leg or hip and walked with a cane, a deterrent which seemed to handicap her not at all as she marched up and down the steep hillsides. One had the impression of enthusiasms and ideas ready to boil out at any provocation, and also of tremendous warmth and incandescent intelligence.

During an evening lecture she told us that she began every day in prayer, and she then described her prayer life to us. She talked about "affirmative prayer" as "the ego in relationship to the will of God in the moment." It is different from meditation, which involves going down into oneself. Prayer involves an I-Thou relationship, whereas meditation is either I or Thou, referring to messages from the deeper self, which sometimes seem to reflect one's own unconscious, and sometimes reflect the Collective Unconscious. Prayer is different from the analytic process. It is the act of "selling all" and must be repeated over and over, bringing more and more of the "all" to the process. There must be reorientation every morning, a willingness to be open to all alternatives and to act on the best value. One must ask oneself, "Why am I doing this?" and answer oneself, "Because I am following an invitation to Life and want to have the most creative response."

She went on to note that one can begin prayer without knowing oneself, but the more one knows of one's "inner rooms" the better, since God "owns the house," so to speak. "If I am really doing what God wants of me, I am living with meaning. There is a pattern and God manifests in the situation and in my psyche." How? "One finds one's own way and one's own symbols. One 'rehearses the day' (psychiatrist Fritz Kunkel's idea) so that one attempts to serve the will of God in imagination." Elizabeth suggested that prayer gets deeper and deeper as one knows more about one's self. It includes finding the self, but is more than finding the self.

She quoted, "I am created for the sake of consciousness and God wants to become something through me," and also, "Man was created for the sake of choice" (from the Jewish Cabala). A person's initial commitment is a big thing (there was, at Four Springs, a great emphasis on Jesus' concept of the Narrow Gate), but then the daily prayers give a framework for the unconscious psyche. One should remember that each day is virginal and one should establish rituals. One has to arouse a sense of presence in order to respond to the Thou searching for each of us. She quoted Fenelon who said, "O God, pray yourself into me."

As I review my notes about this lecture I am aware of deep puzzlement over why this moving insight was not incorporated into the structure of the seminar. Perhaps the influence of others diluted Elizabeth's vision in this regard. I have a sense that Four Springs became more self-consciously anti-church and thus less specifically devotional as its history progressed. But the insight regarding the relationship between prayer and knowledge of the inner self is the one positive teaching from Four Springs that remains with me and merges with my prayer experiences during the Nineteenth and at Shalem.

When I look back on the sixteen days at Four Springs, what stands out in my memory? Above all, subtle authoritarianism disguised as "openness" and their nonrecognition of this. They talked a lot about "owning your projections"—not dumping (projecting out) your unresolved conflicts. But while they saw authoritarianism and dogmatism in all the organized churches, they failed to see it in their own midst. I also remember an unpleasant sense of my life being totally out of my control. The isolation, the case conferences, and the long periods of silence all conspired to enhance the cumulative effect. A rigid structure was designed to manage the outcome of the sixteen days. In this respect the leadership was outspoken. "Don't judge the process until it's finished," we were told, and I suppose my willingness to stay out the sixteen days came partly from curiosity to see if there would be some marvelous reversal toward the end. But as we approached the

Passion story and the Resurrection accounts in the gospels, my internal tension increased.

"What will you do with that material?" I asked one of the staff.

"I'm sure you already know," he replied.

"No happy surprises?" I said hopefully.

"I doubt it," was his response.

At the last session we were invited to talk about our experience at Four Springs. I had gotten so many messages about my unpleasant animus that I was by then fighting to control my hostility, and as a result I had developed such severe arthritis in my right hand that for a few days writing, my primary mode of expression, was almost impossible for me. It is not a symptom I have ever had before or since. So the opportunity for written reflection came at a time when my pent-up thoughts and feelings were causing me serious distress.

In the beginning I tried to be reasonable and unemotional, but before more than a few words were out of my mouth I lost control, and sixteen days' worth of unexpressed thoughts and feelings came boiling out. I talked about what seemed to me to be shocking ignorance of what is going on in much of contemporary Christendom, about the manipulation of scriptural material, about propaganda masquerading as education, about their absurd stance that if everyone would engage in personal depth analysis the problem of evil would disappear, and about astonishing self-righteousness regarding the sins of the world, unaccompanied by risk taking of any significant kind. I remember saying through my tears that I was not aware that any of the leadership were putting their lives on the line in Central America the way many of the church people I knew were doing. I think I may even have alluded to the use of Four Springs as a recruiting ground for the private analytic practices of the leadership, a lack of tact which must particularly have endeared me to the staff.

This outburst took place on the morning of the day in which we departed. I expected to be treated as a pariah and I was indeed aware that people at first didn't know what to say to me. But over the lunch period, and during the van ride into San Francisco with seven other participants, people started reacting to me. Friends expressed concern over my distress. "You said a lot of things I had been thinking but didn't have the nerve to say," was the tenor of many comments. During that ride to town there was an odd sense of escape. For several hours we could be as disloyal to Four Springs as we liked. We gossiped and unloaded ideas which we thought were peculiar to each of us alone, as though we had been in a "bugged" environment in which traitorous notions would have been punished. During those last few hours, I felt more genuine communication with many people than I had experienced during the entire time I was at Four Springs.

PART THREE:

The Country
of Life

CHAPTER 11

In Bondage to Sin

I did not expect to come into the Country of Life with sin on my mind. I guess I had envisioned my transformed face wearing the sort of blissed-out expression that the TM people seemed to exhibit. In my innocence I thought that in the Country of Life I would be peaceful, calm, and unafraid, a sort of Christian Dali Lama. But after four years of encounters with a variety of Christians in a variety of places, it finally occurred to me that Christianity expects us to struggle with our dual nature. So confrontation with evil seems to me to be one of the most useful, if surprising, results of my pilgrimage—a "desert experience," so to speak.

My time at Four Springs was troubling on many levels. If, indeed, evil was present, it apparently rode in on the best of good intentions. One usually connects evil with sin, but the only serious sin I could identify at Four Springs was, as I said, hubris (arrogant pride). And if kindness, intelligence, beauty, and self-discipline are virtues, then I can see that my assessment may have been a projection, just as the staff suggested. But what was I projecting? What unacceptable part of myself was I seeing in them? As I now reflect on the sixteen days at Four Springs I ask myself: Could hubris be my problem as well as theirs? And is hubris connected to the judgmentalism I identified during the Ignatian Exercises?

"What is your worst fault?" It is a sobering question. In encounter groups the question was sometimes phrased like this: "Consider the worst thing you ever did. What would people think of you if they knew?" The point was that our sense of "badness" (never "sin") is often based on our embarrassment about imagined personal shortcomings.

"I sometimes spanked my toddler son with a hairbrush," I once reluctantly admitted. "It came close to being a beating. He was a willful kid and his energy wore me out. I was an invalid. I didn't have any spare energy and sometimes I just couldn't get through to him."

My group flooded me with reassurance. "You didn't mean to hurt him, you were just stretched too thin," said a friend, her voice tender with sympathy. "But he turned out okay, right?" Other group members were eager to demonstrate that what I did was symptomatic of an impossible situation, "wrong" in one sense but not "sinful."

But, of course, I did mean to hurt him—that's why I was hitting him. And when I search my soul I can see how child-beating—even "spanking" with a hairbrush—is a first step on the road to something very much worse. Sometimes, when I give my imagination full rein, a potential murderer appears, lurking inside me. Sometimes, when I am kept awake by teenagers playing their car radios full blast outside my bedroom window, I envision myself kneeling beside the open window with a machine gun, ambushing them. I can even, if I let myself, imagine myself as a torturer, a slave owner, a Nazi . . . there are very few atrocities I cannot picture myself committing. And I'm convinced that this is true of most people. Why else was the movie *Pulp Fiction* such a success? Why do kids play war? Why is there so much violence on television?

We once debated all this in a discussion group at the Congregational church I was then attending, a church that prided itself on careful thinking. "I believe in progress," one member asserted. "I think, over all, God is leading the world into better and better understanding and behavior."

"I agree," said someone else. "I believe that science will eventually eliminate what we call evil, which results, in my opinion, from ignorance."

I was skeptical. "What about the sorry history of the twentieth century?"

"Well yes, I suppose some bad things have happened. But think how much we've achieved."

Some bad things? We've achieved hydrogen bombs, political chaos, holocausts, and ethnic cleansings in Germany, Russia, China, Cambodia, Africa, and the Balkans, and old-fashioned corruption in much of the world. This did not strike me as "progress."

"Where," I hesitantly asked my progressive friends, "is this so-called progress going to take the world? Will we be part of this heaven on earth? Do you care that probably we'll be long gone?"

My question called forth a challenge. "What about human perfectibility and essential goodness? Isn't civilization built on that idea?" Around the table people nodded agreement. My adversary was encouraged. "Furthermore, is there really such a thing as sin?" she asked. "Isn't the word just used to make people feel guilty? As long as I don't hurt anyone, shouldn't I be able to do what I want?"

"And if you do hurt someone?"

"Then I've made a mistake, or I'm still immature. I'm weak or afraid or I need to work on my anger, but I don't see how it helps anything to call it sin."

Whoo-eee.

I grew up during the Second World War, so the problem of sin is tied to a troubling question for me. Would I have collaborated with the Nazis had I lived in Germany during the thirties and forties? Would I have noticed the unexplained smoke coming from those odd "factories" on the edge of town? How hard would my heart have turned out to be when my neighbors began to disappear?

"Well," the apologists for the no-sin school argue, "you would have been scared. It's understandable that people wanted to protect themselves."

And if I wasn't scared? I somehow doubt that that would have been my motive. I come from a family of old-fashioned anti-Semites. Jokes about "the yids" were standard dinner table entertainment among my Chicago relatives. Indeed, I come from a family of racists in the broad sense, and I could not now bring myself to transcribe some of the names that black people were called. My Chicago relatives were not scared of anyone. They were amazingly arrogant, convinced that it was they who should set the standards of behavior and ideas for everyone else. If we cannot use the word "sinners" to describe them, what word should we use? I have no doubt that in Nazi Germany they would have been Nazis. One of them once even tried to start an argument with me about whether or not the Holocaust was a fiction made up by the Jews.

I think about mental health and mental illness. Were my Chicago relatives mentally ill? That certainly is an excuse often used by the no-sin people. But they seemed to me to be successful, productive, reasonably happy, attractive, wealthy, influential, and self-confident—a fine definition of mental health by most people's standards.

Sometimes God is used in support of the argument that there is no such thing as sin. "God don't make no junk," a good friend jokingly suggests. But, of course, God do make junk—the Bible is full of stories of the junk that God made. Do we have to conceive of a sinister spoiler such as Satan corrupting creation (it goes without saying that my friend doesn't believe in Satan) or shall we argue that, in a sense, junk is God's way of coercing us to improve ourselves—that the whole of evolution turns on the necessity for created life to deal with junk?

I suggest to my broad-minded friend that in the Bible God seems to be irrational, cruel, impotent, judgmental, and capricious—making junk right and left. I remind her of a television broadcast we watched together in which some bright and successful professionals somewhat smugly argued that they had trouble believing in a God who allowed Cain to get away with murder and who impulsively decided to expunge an unsatisfactory world with a flood. The idea that humanity was proving itself to be remarkably sinful from the very beginning was not a justification in their view. God, it was said with a smile, should have been a good papa. He should have provided a little divine sympathy and understanding; after all, it was unkind of God to put the Tree of the Knowledge of Good and Evil where Adam and Eve could be tempted by it. And when those early "made in His image" creatures made such bad choices, surely divine psychotherapy was called for, not judgment of such a bad-tempered sort.

I had the sense, in listening to this television discussion, of being back with Job, hearing his self-righteous friends explain to him why he had lost all his worldly goods, family, health, and reputation, in spite of his impeccable character. There had to be a logical explanation, an explanation that made sense. But finally, after logic, reason, tradition, and piety had failed to assuage Job's fury at God, a Voice out of the whirlwind thundered, "Where were you when I laid the foundation of the world?"

Good question. I remind my junk-denying friend about the Voice from the whirlwind. "God is not," I argue, "a liberal American intellectual, any more than God was a self-righteous intellectual Hebrew in Job's time." What I do not say is that we don't have any more idea why God does or does not interfere with human life than my dog has an idea why I won't let him pee in the house or bite the mailman. Supreme illogic on both counts from a doggy point of view; all he is trying to do is mark his territory and protect his loved ones.

I have come to believe that sin is a simple idea that any ten-year-old kid can understand perfectly. "Sometimes I'm bad." When my ten-year-old son stole a friend's baseball glove and then lied to me about it, he was in touch with something bad inside himself. It kept him awake at night, weeping with guilt. When I failed to visit my eighty-five year old stepmother-in-law in the nursing home because I did not like her, even though I knew she wanted to see me, I was in touch with something bad inside myself. It had nothing to do with mental illness.

My son the thief rationalized that maybe his friend didn't want the baseball glove and that was why he left it on our front porch.

Anyway, "finders keepers." It was the friend's fault that my son had this nifty glove. However, I am proud to say that after a while even a ten-year-old like himself was no longer able to buy that excuse. The truth was, he wanted the glove. Period. He had a nice sturdy conscience (superego) and he was willing to say, in effect, "I am a sinner." And I, playing God as mothers do, said to him, in effect, "Because you have confessed and repented, your sins are forgiven." How much better was that outcome than some nonsense about his being a good boy who had made a mistake.

The old Lutheran confession states that we are in bondage to sin. My psychotherapist self may cringe at that nasty word, but truth is truth. Guilt is good. Guilt alerts us to our sins. Guilt causes us to repent and be forgiven by God. The absolute bottom line of Christianity is drawn from this understanding. But the huge splinter in the eye for most secular people is not, I believe, an intellectual problem with theological dogma; it is a discounting of the value of guilt—an unwillingness to fall on their faces and confess themselves to be sinners.

My personal willingness to endure a guilty conscience stems from a teaching about the nature of sin and evil that seems so obvious I wonder it is not taught in grade school. Fritz Perls, the originator of Gestalt therapy, talked about it; the Buddhists talk about it; Carl Jung talked about it; even the Book of Genesis talks about it. We live in a world of polar opposites: up-down, hard-soft, good-bad, light-dark—everything in the material world contains its opposite. Yin and yang, beginnings and endings, birth and death, good and evil. When God created the world, God created light out of darkness, earth was separated from water, and time was divided into days. No pattern of reality exists except as contrast. When people talk scornfully about "dualism," as though there were some other way of existing in the universe, I wonder what they know that the rest of us do not.

In my heart I am a liberal evangelical for precisely this reason: the evangelical churches provide a framework for the syndrome of confession, repentance, and forgiveness that I believe is basic to

Christian discipleship. It is astonishing to me that some churches still call themselves Christian without any reference to sin. A church I once attended never spoke of sin. We could not sing "Amazing Grace" because the assistant minister objected to the phrase "a wretch like me." As a member of that church, if I felt guilty about something I would, I presume, have been therapized or euphemized out of my guilt. There would have been, in that setting, no place for me humbly to confess my sin: not in the church service itself, and not in individual counseling.

What is my worst fault? My own darkest fault—the aspect of myself that makes me most susceptible to sin—as I said earlier, I reluctantly identify as judgmentalism. But judgmentalism can be the dark side of what is sometimes referred to as "discernment"—identifying good and evil—one of the gifts of the Spirit spoken of by Saint Paul. So my judgmentalism has a dual nature; it is both gift and temptation. The gift of discernment sometimes gives me helpful sensitivity, but it also causes me to be a prig sometimes (often?). But whether as sensitivity or self-righteousness, this gift of the Spirit apparently is not optional. I cannot be rid of it. It is like an unwelcome spotlight, or a bad smell, or a persistently nagging voice whispering "Uh, oh" into my ear.

I try to soften my judgments in the style I learned from my psychology books, and I try to be easier on myself. But sin is an adversary with whom I am well acquainted and therefore I try also to wear "the full armor of God," as it is phrased in the letter to the Ephesians—to shield myself with God's goodness and an unyielding affirmation of my Christian faith.

CHAPTER

12

A Sacred Heart

A freezing early-morning fog glazes the wooden steps on the walk down to the food cabin for breakfast. I tread cautiously so as not to slip onto my bottom. I think ruefully that my old bones are not as resilient as those of my fellow-authors. It is 1997 and together with twenty or so other Christian writers I am spending a late fall weekend at a rural Presbyterian retreat center north of Detroit. It has been seven years since I last immersed myself in a Christian setting of this kind and I am again reminded of my always dangerous judgmentalism. "Pious amateurs," I thought to myself when the brochure first arrived, sarcastically discounting the term "Christian writers." After all, I was (ahem) a published author. But by now my earlier pridefulness has been replaced by humility as the weekend sweeps me into Presbyterian faithfulness and hard work.

However, I am brought up short during the final meeting. One of the participants—I will call her Janet—describes a retreat she recently organized entitled "Friendship with Jesus." She is puzzled by the lack of men in attendance. Impulsively, I suggest that perhaps the topic seemed silly to them. Janet seizes on the word "silly" and asks me to say more. "Well," I say, "maybe the idea of friendship with an imaginary character named Jesus seems sentimental and foolish. I think there's always a danger that religion itself may seem silly to some people."

Janet is deeply offended. "I feel attacked. How can you use that word 'silly'? Do you think everyone should be an intellectual like you? The rest of us are just silly?" By now Janet is in tears.

I am filled with remorse. "No, no, no," I assert desperately. "I was just trying to answer your question about the lack of men's participation." But Janet is not to be appeased. "I worked hard on that retreat," she stammers through her tears. "Most people don't view Christianity the way you do. Do you think only intellectuals are sincere Christians?" Now she is seriously angry.

Oh dear. I try to think how to respond. "I guess you're right. I do have an intellectual approach to religion." I hesitate as I try to think why this is so. "You know," I add, "where I grew up, religion was ridiculed. So if I wasn't going to park my brains at the door I had to convince myself that religion wasn't silly and in particular that Christianity wasn't silly."

But her anger causes me to question myself. Am I, as she accuses me of being, merely an intellectual Christian? Setting aside the word "merely," I'm not apologetic to be an intellectual Christian. After all, "thinking about it" is the convert's burden and I am a convert. Faith is not infused in my bones as it might have been were I brought up as a Christian. My parents and my education stressed the irrationality of religion, so my intellect had to be dealt with.

What I didn't say to Janet, but say privately to myself, is that "birthright Christians" (a Quaker term) seem often to skid away from intellectual questions altogether, as if any serious discussion would undermine their faith. "Let's keep religion and science separate," or, "I'm not going to think about that." But my own intellect has been hugely important in grounding me firmly in Christianity. Setting aside theological arguments, the most important outcome of my adventures has been the enlarging of my worldview so that alternative realities now seem plausible. Not that I have had out-of-body experiences or encounters with little large-eyed aliens. Rather, over the years, personal doubts about conventional scientific wisdom have accumulated.

Now I'm going to admit my credulousness by admitting that I believe in UFOs. My first serious doubts about the scientific viewpoint were triggered by a front-page headline in the Ann Arbor News sometime late in the 1950s: "UFO Lands in Dexter Field." The small town of Dexter is about five miles from the house where I then lived. According to the newspaper story, a farmer and his teenage son had seen a large metallic object sitting in the field behind their house. I don't recall if they watched it take off and leave, or if later it simply was gone, but the point was that they saw it clearly. They were able to provide a drawing and an exact description. Of course, the story created a brief sensation—some college students in a nearby town later claimed to have seen it overhead and an astronomy professor from Ohio State, Allen Hynek, was commissioned by the U.S. government to study the event. Hynek announced that the sightings were caused by "swamp gas" (a conclusion he later admitted was ridiculous) and it seemed clear that he was expected, a priori, to dismiss the event out of hand. "It can't be true, so it isn't true." So much for science, I thought.

But for me the most interesting aspect of this event was the reaction of my next-door neighbor, a psychologist and one of the smartest people I knew. "What do you think about all that?" I asked her during our regular coffee time together. "I don't," she said dismissively. "I've got too many other things on my mind." Hmmm. It contradicted her view of reality so it wasn't worth consideration. And along the same line, the farmer's house was soon pelted with eggs and rotten tomatoes. He said he wished he had kept the whole business to himself. Apparently other people also were upset to have their views of reality challenged. It had to do, I later concluded, with what are called "paradigms"—the lenses through which we view experience.

Through the years other experiences caused me to be skeptical about the scientific viewpoint. In the early sixties, during one of my monumental colds—"Lord, just let me die!"—I read about the Nobel Prize winner Linus Pauling's contention that massive doses of vitamin C could alleviate cold symptoms. In desperation, and being too sick even to venture out of the house, I commissioned Herb to buy me a bottle of vitamin C. When he came back he said all he could find were fifty-milligram tablets. I seemed to recall from my reading that one should start with a thousand-milligram dose, so desperately I washed twenty tablets down my throat. I did it anxiously—would that much vitamin C hurt me?—and without much hope that it would help. I had, after all, tried nostrums like antihistamines no avail. But to my amazement the next day I was much better. Yes, I still had a cold, but the awful rawness was gone.

So I tried vitamin C with the next cold, and the next, and over the years vitamin C has revolutionized my experience of colds. However, my medical friends argued, don't I know about the halo effect? About placebos? I expected to get better so I did. But though eventually I read about "scientific" experiments with vitamin C, they revealed little palliative effect. Why was that, when my own experience was so positive? I finally noticed that these experiments seemed to use doses much smaller than those Dr. Pauling had recommended. It occurred to me that the experimenters didn't expect vitamin C to work so, in a sense, they "rigged" the experiments.

So much, I again thought, for science. Apparently, science is not intellectually neutral. I began to notice other examples of ways in which scientific experiments were subtly rigged to prove what was already accepted wisdom. Not always, of course—thank God for penicillin—but often enough to free me to entertain some unproved propositions and possibilities. As the New Age writer Lawrence LeShan has noted, "The impossible can't happen." That is, if something has been observed and reported, it begs the question to dismiss it as "impossible." (Or "coincidence," which seems to be another all-purpose explanation.)

Finally, I encountered a philosophic idea that crystallized for me the vague discomfort I had begun to feel about scientific explanations. During a class at St. John's Seminary during the late eighties, a visiting scholar began his lecture with the assertion, "No one knows what reality is." He shook his finger at us. "No one," he repeated, anticipating our skepticism. "We only know that we exist. That's all. All the rest of our assumptions about reality are only opinions." He went on to suggest that whether we imagine the rest of the world like a great cosmic dream, or whether we are seeds planted in time to grow and develop as best we can, or whether we are simply accidents of fate, we can only guess. Even mystical experiences may be hallucinations. He was talking, of course, about paradigms. That again. We view existence through our own particular (not to say peculiar) lenses.

I cannot be intellectually honest with myself, cannot proceed into theology and faith, without a grounding in existential philosophy. And with the idea of paradigms I am finally able to put on new reality glasses, to view the world through new lenses. "New eyes to see," Jesus called it. Suddenly, I realize that this is precisely what Jesus was talking about. Above all, Christianity requires us to view the world in a new way.

But is my latter-day Christianity simply an intellectual response to overwhelming "why" questions, a defensive strategy enabling me to cope with death in an otherwise unbearable void? I return to my emotional interchange with Janet. Am I merely an intellectual Christian? No. Although changing the way I view reality has been important to my Christian faith, even back in my hospital bed something more profound was going on. Why did I love communion so much? Why did the poetry of the liturgy bring tears to my eye?. Something mysterious was happening.

Not until I finally experienced psychotherapy did I realize what that "something" was. Not until my subconscious psyche was freed and affirmed, as it was with Mrs. Mason, did I escape the tyranny of my intellect. Until then I had lived in my head—"that rocky desert," as I once called it. But during those quiet hours, in Mrs. Mason's tranquil basement office, long-repressed images and feelings came pouring out. Beyond thought I began to experience a mysterious happiness and peace that was clearly connected to my religious faith. Somehow my heart was freed from its bondage to my mind. Christians refer to "the sacred heart," meaning an inner awareness of God that stands by itself—illogical, emotional, filled with goodness and beauty—a spiritual center not dependent on thought. I realize I did not think God's sacred presence into my heart—I presume no one does. It happened when I got out of the way. That, I have learned, is what the word "grace" means.

I unexpectedly found God through my subconscious psyche. In the code language of symbols, dreams, metaphors, music, nature, and scripture, God spoke to me. To be sure, I had planted myself in an environment filled with God's images and words. Although I had been afraid that my yearning for God and my passion for theology would turn out to be my major neuroses, instead I discovered that these came from my absolute wellspring. Whether with guided daydreams in Kansas, meditation at Shalem, morning prayer during the Ignatian exercises, or silent worship at Pendle Hill, I discovered that when I freed my mind from worldly concerns the Inner Light was there. The poet John Keats tells us: "Beauty is truth, truth beauty, that is all ye know on earth, and all ye need to know." Beauty and truth, I have come to believe, find resonance in our sacred hearts—in awareness of our spirituality.

But why, my New Age friends ask me, cannot one be spiritual without belonging to a church? My answer is that spirituality by itself is not necessarily beneficent. We all know people who describe themselves as "spiritual." They believe they are in touch with a power beyond themselves and in order to keep this esoteric knowledge pure and unsullied they pick and choose from a variety of spiritual practices that appeal to them—sweat lodges, the I-Ching, meditation, past-life therapies, guided imagery, and so forth—practices that are deliberately removed from any institutional church. They pick and choose from among a variety of traditions without any commitment or risk taking.

I myself was suspicious of the institutional church for many years. I thought I was expressing my spirituality by doing God's will through my social work. I used to keep this quotation by William Blake on my kitchen bulletin board: "He who would do good must do it in minute particulars. General good is the plea of the scoundrel, the hypocrite, and the flatterer." I meant that quote as a moral lesson for my social worker self, remembering my propensity for avoiding smelly home visits and whiny clients in favor of reforming the agency intake procedures. But (though it took me a while to see this) it applies equally well to my religious self. Philosophy and theology were fun, safe, and easy. The truth is that I was afraid that the "minute particulars" of church membership would disillusion me. I was afraid that I knew too much to be associated with those unenlightened people who had not studied theology as I had done. Furthermore, my high-minded attitude toward church membership very much resembled my early attitude toward therapy. In both cases I worried there might be nothing of substance there—that church membership might kill my faith and psychotherapy might kill my psyche. It was, I finally realized, my judgmental self at its most judgmental.

But without my noticing that it was happening, the church people I got to know—during my pilgrimage, in small groups, in committee meetings, in women's circle meetings, and in Sunday school classes—mysteriously filled my heart and melted my loneliness. At the Lutheran church I belonged to for ten years I became acquainted with wonderful second-generation German-American women like our old housekeeper, Miss Lutz. They grew up on farms as Herb's mother did. They had lined faces and gnarled hands and patiently cooked for funeral lunches and Lenten suppers. I was amazed to find these same women present at the introductory meditation class I once conducted, and at spirituality workshops. They were more curious, open-minded, and generous than I ever could have imagined. I have a mental image of one arthritic older woman carefully taking off her shoes and slowly lowering herself onto the carpeted floor of the fancy church lounge in order to try out some simple yoga exercises. The men too were a revelation—earnest believers, hard workers, passionate citizens of the church.

This said, I remain perplexed by my own church membership history—or lack of it. I have drifted between the Episcopalians, where I began, the Lutherans, Quakers, Congregationalists, Catholics, Christian Reformed, and Presbyterians. Each has offered me some wonderful gifts. From the Episcopalians I received the gift of the traditional mass, the old Book of Common Prayer, and C. S. Lewis. With the Lutherans I experienced belonging and fellowship. With the Quakers I encountered simplicity, silence, kindness, and awesome responsibility. At the Congregational Church I reconnected with my family's origin (my grandfather was a trustee and there is a church window given in my grandparents' names) and had the pleasure of supporting Herb's newfound church membership. The Catholics have seemed to me more deeply Christian than anyone else, and I will always cherish the many places and communions I shared with them but, as I said, Catholicism is too foreign a land for me ever to feel at home there. At the opposite extreme, my summer visits to a little Reformed church in Northern Michigan filled me with song and wonderful fundamentalism. And the Presbyterians are currently honoring my intellectual proclivities and again filling my religious life with music. I continue to feel the hot breath of the Hound of Heaven and I continue to believe that if I am attentive, I will be led.

I am sitting in the basement of Zion Lutheran Church on a Wednesday evening in November 1997. I have not been in this building for more than two years and I am startled by the power of my reaction. My friend Mary has (again) dragged me here to the midweek communion service because, she tells me, a wonderful guest will be preaching. We sit on folding chairs at one end of the cavernous room. A table on a small wooden platform serves as the altar, on which a pottery chalice and plate wait politely under white coverings. A wooden cross stands silent watch behind them. No bulletin or service book is available to order the service.

The small group is welcomed by the popular new pastor, someone I have not met before, who has bravely taken on the task of rescuing Zion from its troubled history. He reads a portion of the lectionary for the week and explains that their guest preacher was at the last minute unable to be there, so the lectionary offered the easiest basis for his sermon. Then informally he offers us, as he says, a "riff" on the text: Christians as salt and yeast, Christians as an "island people." It is a wonderful idea which I have always found profoundly moving. Tonight I find it speaks to my occasionally alienated heart with words of great comfort.

At the conclusion of the informal sermon the young lay assistant intones the introduction to communion. I find I can still repeat the responses from memory. Back and forth, back and forth, invocation and response, invocation and response. We are invited to come forward "in the usual way" and the pastor breaks the pita bread into tiny pieces as he says, "This is my body which is given for you." I find myself in line waiting my turn to commune. I take a little flat piece of bread from the pastor's hand, dip it into the cup, murmur "amen," and return to my chair.

In how many settings have I done this, beginning with that introductory communion in my hospital bed? I remember my first Catholic communion in the chapel at St John's Seminary. I felt sure I had "Lutheran" stamped in Protestant ink on my forehead; the priest would take one look and withdraw the cup with an accusatory frown. That, of course, did not happen. In fact, only once have I been intimidated into not participating in communion, in a small Missouri Synod Lutheran church in upper Michigan. (The advanced warnings about nonmembers defiling the Lord's Supper were so dark and stern that I found myself glued to my seat—I was, in this church's view, the wrong variety of Lutheran.)

I find tonight, as I have often found before, that my heart is most engaged when God manages to bypass my busy mind. "I always thought Christians were cannibals," once noted a Jewish friend, referring to communion. She meant it as a joke—of course she knew better and she liked to tweak me—but I think now about what she said. The body and blood of Christ. I do not require that they be solely commemorative, even though the idea of the "actual presence" seems a bit macabre. It is the very irrationality of communion, the primitive symbolism, the deeply unconscious connection with our own body and blood, that cause me to long for communion, to feel dry and deprived without it.

We stand and sing the hymn, "Blessed Assurance." I am aware that music again engages my heart irrationally. "Blessed assurance, Jesus is mine. Oh what a foretaste of glory divine." It does not make a lot of sense if you put your rational mind to it. I think of Christmastime and "Messiah." "As by man came death, so too by man came the Resur-rection." How can anyone encounter those words without hearing in imagination that triumphal music?

The service is over. "Go in peace," says the pastor, as he blesses us with the sign of the cross. "Serve the Lord." I stand, look around, and greet old friends from my Zion past. My heart is filled for a while with goodness and beauty and truth.

13

Last Days

It is August in Northern Michigan. The late season sun barely warms us as we pull five folding chairs into a tight circle on the dewy grass where our vacation book club regularly meets. We all are saddened by the passing of another summer and the analogy to growing old occurs to someone. Idly we speculate on what it feels like to get old.

"I hope I don't have to hang around," says elegant Mary Ann, pulling her tan Bleyle sweater more tightly around her. Tomorrow she goes back to Des Moines where her eighty-five-year-old mother is becoming increasingly frail and increasingly demanding. "I dread the whole business," she notes. "My mother does nothing but complain. What's the point?" And then she adds sharply, "When I don't have any more to contribute—when I'm not growing spiritually—then I think it's time for me to check out. Let's hear it for Doctor Kevorkian." She half means it.

I feel chilled and my self-righteousness kicks in. "It seems to me that courage itself provides a kind of growth," I suggest somewhat pompously. Mary Ann nods politely, but I can see by her reaction that courage in the face of increasing incapacity doesn't strike her as anything she's interested in for herself.

I persist. "Maybe caring for old people has lessons to teach us. Like compassion and kindness."

"Yuk," she says. "My mother should suffer so I can be kind? I don't think so."

I think to myself that some grim contemporary command-ments apply here: "Thou shalt not suffer any pain," and "Thou shalt be in control." But then a hopeful idea occurs to me, and I hesitantly offer it to my controlling friend with her decrepit mother. "Maybe 'emotional floating' can be a substitute for a take-charge life. Maybe, if we just tread water, life will surprise us." (What I don't say is that God might speak to us if we relax, calm down, and listen.)

Only small blonde Joan, thirty-five and fighting metastatic breast cancer, understands my idea. "Sometimes we can't be in control," she reminds everyone. But apparently that's too alarming a thought to take seriously, positive thinking being the dogma of the day. However, I wonder if the price my friend will eventually pay for her passion for control will be depression and panic when the consequence of not dying young finally catches up with her. Dislike of the old will then become dislike of herself.

I remembered an elderly friend who, in her late seventies, moved to our town to be near her son. An intensely faithful, lifelong Lutheran, she was still full of vigor and enthusiasm. When she joined our Lutheran church she chose to become part of the women's circle I belonged to, a circle comprised of women between thirty and fifty. She was by far the oldest woman at our monthly meetings.

Within a few months I began to hear grumbling. "There are plenty of circles for women her age," someone said. "We don't want to listen to her stories about the old days," said someone else. "She just doesn't fit in," said yet a third person. But my impression was that she added a lot of experience, wisdom, and Christian faithful-ness to our discussions. So once, when I was driving her home, out of curiosity I asked her if she had tried other circles. "Oh yes," she said. "But the ladies are all so old. I find it depressing."

I hardly knew where to begin in considering the levels of ageism in that remark. My friend's dislike of women of her own generation eventually resulted in her remaining in a small, cluttered apartment long after some sort of retirement facility would have made her life easier. The corresponding ageism of the women in our circle was even more startling because one would think these professedly Christian women would be sensitive to the implications of their judgments about elderly friends. Did they believe that they themselves would not be rejected by the young when they were seventy-five? Or did they plan to stay so deceptively "young" that no one would notice?

I, of course, am not immune to ageism either. One day I put on a one-piece jumpsuit without a waistline because I have developed a serious belly. It was a roaringly hot summer day and I delivered myself a lecture about my belly. "Yes, I know this outfit makes me look seven months pregnant, but why do I care? I am seventy years old. No one loves me for my figure and this is the coolest thing I own." But it startles me to see in the mirror the matron I have become, and I have to continually remind myself that old women are a part of life's montage fully as much as young women; thank God for Angela Lansbury on TV, who sometimes even has a bit of a tummy herself.

I myself am now old. The secret I keep hidden is that I truly don't mind. Recently I heard an apparently self-confident, gray-haired man, with elegant character wrinkles and perfect teeth, assert that he never believed people when they said they didn't mind growing older because, "of course everyone minds growing older. Why wouldn't they? They have something so much better to compare it to—being young." Setting aside the observation that growing older had obviously treated him very kindly indeed, I noted to myself that his assumptions about old age seemed suspect for several reasons, not least of which is the fact that not everyone loved being young.

I, for one, did not—not when I was a child and not when I was a young adult. Being young meant to me being poor, tired, depressed, ill, and psychologically insecure. Being young meant helplessness, too many small children, zero energy, and continuous infections of one sort or another. Thinking back, I realize there is almost nothing about being young that I would want to relive. My high school classmates have recently begun having yearly get-togethers and are mystified by my annual refusals to attend. I recently bought some tapes of old World War II songs and discovered I couldn't make myself listen to them. When my husband entertains himself with slides of our forty-years-ago life, I find something else to do.

Old age, I have concluded, is just reverse adolescence. There are frequent surprises when I look in the mirror now, just as there were then, and my emotional reaction is also similar—physical life on a bell curve, so to speak. Unfortunately, the resemblance to adolescence also recalls the old familiar dislike of my body, "my body, the enemy," as I once told a sensitivity group, though truthfully, my body is no worse than most people's. But I do find it hard to get used to the fact that, unlike with adolescence, one does not grow out of getting old.

However, I agree with my sister that this is a time to be a "wise person"—whatever that means. (In practice I observe it to mean that everything reminds me of something that happened years ago, about which I am happy to pontificate. Sigh.) "Life," the wise person I plan to be would say, "is not about being young and beautiful. Life is about living." (How's that for a truism?) Life is amazing, full of surprises, always dangerous. I plan to see it through with as much curiosity and courage as the Lord will let me have. So there!

I still think about death, the more so since my mother died recently. I wonder what it is like to die, and what if anything happens afterward. But my death phobia has gradually faded away and I'm not terrified of the prospect as I once was. I realize too that I think about God all the time, as if there is a continual presence with me. Someone said to me once, "My whole life is a prayer," and I knew just what he meant. It sounds excessively pious to say it, but my sense is that every now and then I look around and feel the tiniest awareness of God in everything. In fact, I sometimes feel like apologizing to God for those times when I am not paying attention. It surprises me (I seem to be surprised by a lot of things) that I feel so certain of my religious underpinnings. That certainty seems to surprise other people as well, but I guess it is my reward for having given the whole business so much thought over the years.

My parents, of course, avoided God right up to the bitter end, even when they were staring into the wrong end of the gun barrel. (Though my mother evolved a truly weird version of Christianity from watching the TV evangelist Frederick Price.) And, of course, my parents did not believe in funerals. When you are dead, you are dead, and the living should get on with it. When Mother died, my sister and I arranged to have her cremated as she had requested and that, we knew, should have been that. We knew that Mother had not arranged a funeral for our dad after he died in 1972; his ashes were (theoretically) sprinkled over the ocean by a commercial pilot who contracted for such services—or so she said.

Not surprisingly, my life has not been full of funerals. The "don't think about it" philosophy of death I talked about earlier extends to funerals as well. If there is a funeral, you have to think about death. I occasionally notice this philosophy reflected in obituaries of my parents' friends: "Cremation has occurred" and then no announcement of any sort of memorial service. Even at the Congregational Church they are not called "funerals," they are called "services of remembrance," and I am reminded that "life after death" in that theology refers to "living on in the memory of one's friends." I think sardonically that life after death has a limited duration under those circumstances, given what happens to most memories. It strikes me as a pathetic idea.

I don't know how to behave at a funeral, and the very idea of a body in a casket still causes me to have an anxiety attack. But my ideal funeral would be modeled on the service for Maynard Klein, longtime choir director at Interlochen and the University of Michigan, "Uncle Maynard" as he was fondly known for many years. His family put a small notice in the Ann Arbor paper asking those who had ever sung in one of Maynard's choirs to come early to the church for the occasion. More than one hundred people showed up to sing in that memorial choir, and at the service the church rang with the hymns and chorales that Maynard had loved. I cannot imagine a more wonderful salute to a life well lived.

I think there could not be a more insulting and blasphemous ending for anyone's life than a departure without a send-off. Of course, having no funeral makes a certain amount of sense if you are a secular materialist—though not a lot, in my judgment, since even in a harshly materialistic universe there can be secular tributes to those we have loved. So three months after Mother's death, and acknowledging our parents' skepticism and dislike of fuss, Gretchie and I planned a family gathering and graveside service in honor of both our parents—for ourselves, if not for them. We invited those of our large extended family who we thought would be interested, and much to our surprise nearly thirty people came from all over the country. I reserved rooms at the local Sheraton and we planned a fancy lunch at the Gandy Dancer, Ann Arbor's converted railroad station-restaurant, of which all of us have many poignant memories. Afterward we all went together to the lovely hillside cemetery where most of our forebears are buried.

To be sure, there was only a marble gravestone bearing both our parents' names (for our dad it was a "cenotaph," meaning a monument without physical remains) and decorated by a carved rose designed by artist Gretch as a symbol of Dad's gardens. A small wooden box contained Mother's ashes and I was supposed to place it reverently into the small grave. But when I knelt beside the hole it was so deep I was afraid of falling in—luckily, the mortuary man in attendance had longer arms. I then read a short tribute, a nephew spoke of his memories of our parents, and our friend Dorothy Lenz, representing the Congregational Church, offered a prayer. Afterward people wandered off over the hill to find the graves of other family members in that cemetery of many memories. I suppose we will never see most of those people again, but many of them thanked us for the opportunity for such a reunion.

Now that they are gone I think about my parents' lives. I think about how captive we are to whatever era we live in, how much we are the fruits of the generational and familial gardens in which we are planted. When my dad was dying I timidly brought up the subject of religion; no doubt I tried to make a little joke out of it.

"Doesn't interest me," was his reply.

"Don't you wonder what happens after you die?" I asked; a blunt question, but Dad and I were often blunt with each other.

"I presume I'll find out when the time comes," he observed.

"Are you afraid?"

"No," he said calmly, "I got over being afraid of death in the Marine Corps. I'm just sorry that I won't be around to see how the grandchildren turn out." He then mused about each grandchild in turn and revealed his latent sexism by noting that my sister's girls would be fine "because they're girls."

I frequently pray for my parents, nudged by my Catholic predilection to pray for those who are gone. Sometimes I'm overcome with sadness for my mother, whose unhappy life ended in a demented old age. I pray for divine pity, because I know that under all that perfectionism and paranoia was a frightened little girl. On the other hand I have never worried about my father's destination in the heavenly kingdom because I have an inexplicable conviction that God will respect his consistent loyalty to the belief system of his generation. He was an intellectually honest person and it seems sad but true that, along with several generations of American intellectuals, he prematurely buried God. Within the framework of his education and upbringing he was straightforwardly honest and brave, and not so rigid as to consider himself an atheist.

"I'm willing to consider evidence that I'm wrong," he said to me at the end of his life.

"Then I'll see you later," I said to him.

Life as a journey, life as a story, or life as a reflection of God—whatever life signifies, it seems to me that a person's life deserves a tribute when it's over. I have even, somewhat presumptuously, planned a funeral for myself and have asked my musician daughter-in-law to arrange for the singing of "Blessed Assurance," "How Great Thou Art," "Crown Him with Many Crowns" and "All Is Well with My Soul."

I hope my spirit can be there.